*MODERN MANAGEMENT SERIES*

# Project Evaluation and Management

*Edited by*

**M.K. Singh**

**Anant Mahadevan**

**DISCOVERY PUBLISHING HOUSE**

**NEW DELHI-110002**

Reprinted - 2019

First Published - 1995

ISBN: 978-81-7141-082-8



**Project Evaluation and Management**

*Published by:*

DISCOVERY PUBLISHING HOUSE PVT. LTD.

4383/4B, Ansari Road, Darya Ganj

New Delhi-110 002 (India)

*Phone*: +91-11-23279245, 23253475; 43596065

*E-mail*: discoverybooksindia@gmail.com

discoverypublishinghouse@gmail.com

*web*: www.discoverypublishinggroup.com

*Printed at:*

Infinity Imaging Systems

Delhi

# *Preface*

The phenomenal growth of commercial enterprises in the past decade or so has been the outcome of an equally remarkable spurt in surplus purchasing power, wage increase, liquidity of holdings and the advent of consumerism impelled by the remarkable technological development during the period. Enterprises and industrial conglomerates, trading services and hire-purchase firms alike have had to move fast to be equal to the opportunities provided by a growing national as well as international market. Industry and enterprises have had to change gears in a big way.

This collection of papers, articles, extracts and contributoins is concerned with the efficient use of available resources—materials, manpower, expertise, incentives and organisational inputs—for efficacious project and operations management in today's competitive albeit liberal and encouraging industrial setting. In an era marked by the liberalisation of industrial controls, backed by appropriate legislation, and the variety of incentives offered to developing industries, especially in the Third World, particularly in India, efficient project and operations management is perhaps the cornerstone of all success of the firm. Attempts have been made in these papers and articles to highlight certain common problem-areas observed in many projects. These problems could trigger cost and time over-runs in a project, if left unresolved. The present compilation keeps this perspective.

In our efforts we have been assisted in generous measure by our many colleagues and friends, professional managers and experts consultants. They would be too numerous to list—suffice it to say that without their guidance these papers and articles would not have been brought together into a cohesive whole. Nonetheless, we feel it our bounden duty to acknowledge the fruitful discussions we have had with Prof. P. Sarveshwar and Dr. Arun Nimbalkar of the Institute of Corporate and Industrial Management, Bombay; Dr. S. Ganesan of the Textile Managers Association, Aurangabad; Shri K. R. Wadhawan of the Centre for Research in Management Sciences, Manila, and Smt. Urvashi Palekar, Documentation Officer, Institute of Corporate Management, Faculty of Economics, University of Lagos, Nigeria.

Excellent computer and secretarial support services were provided by S/Shri Sameer Kak, Arvind Goswami and Raghuraj T. We are grateful to them.

We have attempted to minimise all printing errors, but hasten to add that we alone are responsible for those that still remain.

M. K. Singh
Anant Mahadevan

# *Introduction*

Management may be defined as the process of efficient functioning based on correct choices and actions. However, in the modern world which is increasingly dependant on large organisations, the most significant situations are those which require organisational management. This implies decision and action in a context which is characterised by organised group or collective activity and the goals or objectives towards which the group effort is directed.

These objectives are pursued by managers, who make decisions pertaining to the desired objectives and concerning relationships among resources—the people, money and machines, materials and methods which can be effectively deployed to attain those objectives. Managers then see that their decisions are carried out and that they have the desired effect. When necessary, they use *control actions* to redirect their resources toward the desired objectives. Since managers of large organisations cannot literally to each and every thing that is required as a result of the decisions that are made, organisational management is a process of *working through others* to achieve broad organisational objectives, such as profit or social welfare, or specific objectives such as the development of a new product with success potential of the efficient and time-bound construction of a power plant.

Management may thus be thought of as involving two major elements, *planning* and *control.* These two aspects of management apply to all areas of organised activity, such as the modern large firm represents. Planning involves decisions and actions concerning the future of the organisation. What type of business should be taken up? What kinds of manpower mix will be needed for effective functioning in the 1990s? What impact will increased leisure time have on the utilisation of the contemplated products?

Control involves decisions and actions related to the present organisations. How should production be scheduled to optimise machine-utilisation time? What should be the efficient allocation of workload among various levels of manpower? What mix of newspaper-radio-TV advertising would be best suited to the products?

Every manager is involved to some degree in both planning and control, but the jobs of many managers emphasise the control component. This is, in fact, true of many jobs which have the word 'planning' in their designation. The job of a production planning manager, for instance, is largely control oriented as it stresses the present and the immediate future rather than the long-term future—which is an intrinsic aspect of correct planning.

Many critical aspects of a project are often overlooked in project formulation and design states due to flaws and inadequacies of pre-investment studies, with the result that the project has to be recast drastically. This has been especially observed in countries with resource crunch, such as those in South and South-East Asia. In a few projects set up for the manufacture of plywood, for instance, in a developing South Asian country, it was observed that the project authority after initial logging in the forests, were required to venture deep into the forests where the terrain was found to be difficult and swampy in the monsoon season. This rendered the transport of logs to the nearby river almost impossible. In other seasons, when access into the forest was relatively easy, the river level was too low for effective floating of logs to the plant site. The projects had to switch over to fuel-based transport for this purpose, so that the plant continued to be on stream. The costs of this switching over, however, were so high that many of the projects have turned sick, while some were abandoned altogether. Such and similar problems are inherent in project design and implementation.

What is the single most important component of any successful implementation of a project? To answer this is to state the obvious. In our experience, we would give high marks for the quality of apex-level management. A project management essentially means working towards objectives with resources that are scarce and with and through people. Project management offers excellent opportunities to understand the dynamics of problem-solving. It is not always necessary that we need a consultant to solve serious problems thrown up during implementation. By focussing on the problem itself and drawing on the experiences of the people in the project working on the concerned task, real solutions can emerge.

In a large irrigation project in Gujarat, a leading civil engineering firm, engaged in main canal contract, faced a serious problem of high turnover of skilled heavy vehicle operators. Despite their vigorous efforts, the firm could not hold on to the trained operators who preferred, after their initial experience, to move over to more lucrative employment in Middle East. Consequently, the utilisation of heavy vehicles hired on high rentals was inefficient, which, in turn, impeded the progress in their project execution. A management consultant offered to work out an incentive package to solve this problem, but the owners had no time for such exercise. One day, the project engineer at the site observed that a few adivasi youths from the nearby tribal village were sitting over the idle earthmovers and smoking. When he approached them offering to train them to operate these vehicles, they, after initial hesitation, agreed and reported to work. Within a few weeks, the project owners found, to their pleasant surprise and relief, in those tribal youths a band of dedicated and more efficient operators whose concept of good living did not extend to passports or Middle East, but was confined to plastics and transistors.

The above instance is a case of learning in a project while working on a problem. This is essentially a concept of "action learning", *i.e.*, conforming real issues in real situation and in real time. This, incidentally, is also an excellent tool of management education/development, but this idea is yet to catch up in this part of the world. The thrust of the argument here is that project owners—or for that matter any organisation—should train thier own practising managers to be consultants and perhaps there lies a key to successful project management.

There can never be a single foolproof way to manage/execute a project. The only constants are project owner's abiding commitment and his determination to confront problems and solve them. To reiterate, a good management can conceal a badly conceived project and probably make a success of it, but a good project cannot indefinitely conceal an inadequate management."

The papers in the present compilation are intended as a handbook for a basic understanding of project management in today's highly complex, competitive and international industrial and commercial business. As such, they will, it is hoped, be useful not only to the executive but also the student and scholar of management.

*Contents*

# 1

# PROJECT MANAGEMENT

NARENDRA K. SETHI*

## The Concept

The concept of Project Management underlies a set of principles, methods and techniques that assist in making effective planning for the performance of tasks which are oriented towards the achievement of some objectives. Such a discipline indeed offers a highly effective managerial tool in the sense that its applicability in aspects of scheduling, controlling and re-planning of programmes and projects is primordial.[1]

Its versatility feature is also evident since a broad spectrum of end goals may be achieved with it, such as research, development, construction, and/or installation of hardware; they may also include the development of computer software.[2]

Project Management has a definite mission. It is not simply building systems but to build specific systems. An illustration of this statement is the world of Electronic Data Processing (EDP), in which any kind of system development or programming effort is generally reffered to as a project. A "task

*Dr. Narendra K. Sethi is Professor of Management, St. John's University, New York.

force" is set up to undertake such projects and directive guidelines are duly imparted by "management specialists."

The growth of project management has occurred much as a need to offset certain shortcoming of the traditional functional management, such as lead systems development and relatively ineffective cost and schedule performances. Among its potential benefits are the following[3]:

1. It provides disciplines which ensure thorough project coverage and primary tasks inclusion;
2. Commits responsibility and assures continuity of efforts despite turnover;
3. Determines real time requirements and provides limits for scheduling;
4. Identifies potential problem areas and takes preventive action;
5. Applies management-by-exception principle in reporting;
6. Measures the degree of accomplishment against current scheduled plans and objectives;
7. Facilitates re-scheduling and periodic evaluation; and
8. Captures historical data and provides project models for future planning.

As Kielian says, however, it also presents some drawbacks.[4] These are:

1. Project priorities and competition for talent may interrupt the stability of the organisation and interfere with its long-range interest by upsetting the normal business of the functional organisation;
2. Long-range planning may suffer as the company gets more involved in meeting schedules and fulfilling the requirements of temporary projects; and

3. Shifting people from project to project may disrupt the trainning of new employees and specialists. This may hinder their growth and development within their fields of specialisation.

Project Management, particularly the management of research and development projects, one of the most innovative and complex management dimensions in existence, necessitates the assemblance of a most effective project team.

A first-hand understanding of the activities required to accomplish the project's objective(s) is the key criterion when selecting an organisational model. Once this concept is clear, attention should then be devoted to align the individual organisational elements, such as:

(a) the project team, and its responsibilities,

(b) the project officer, and

(c) the project manager.

It is up to the top management core to select the most appropriate model that fits task demands and scopes.

*Organisational Alternatives*

There are three basic organisational alternatives that can be adopted in the field of Project Management:

1. Pure Project Organisation, where the project participants work directly for the project manager and the latter runs the project as if it were a one-product business enterprise;
2. Pure Functional Organisation, where a multiple-specialised manpower force is grouped together to achieve projects of different nature;
3. Matrix Organisation, composed of both project and functional human force and usually integrated to

tackle large, diversified projects. This pattern of structure is distinctively project-completion oriented, and adapts itself to four different modes in accordance with varying degrees of authority and responsibility taken up by the project manager:

(a) Project manager(s) reports directly to the President or General Manager on a functional basis;

(b) Project manager(s) reports to a Manager of Project Management, who in turn reports to the President or General Manager, on a functional basis;

(c) Project manager(s) linked up to another functional department, but reporting to the President or General Manager, on a functional basis;

(d) Project manager performing staff functions by directly advising the President or General Manager.

Among the several tasks undertaken by project managers, it can certainly be stated that the functions of Planning and Implementation of the plans are pervasive to them.

Within the project environment, plans need to be accommodated to different types of projects which require a diversity of resources as well as performance, under variables or constraints like time, costs and small error margin.

*Cyclical Process*

All these considerations lead to the thinking of Project Management as a cyclical process with step-wise sequences.

The typical planning cycle involves two phases:

(A) Planning Phase which is a three stage achievement:

1. Establishing Programme Objectives: commencing with a statement of work (SOW), standard specifications, and necessary documentation, a Work Breakdown Structure (WBS) is laid out to display the total system with all of its component elements and their respective interaction.
2. Development of the Plans: this entails identification of major interim achievements or milestones which lead to the development of event-logic networks, as described later in this article.
3. Activity-Scheduling: translatión of the generated network into time-schedules and resource constraints, such as expenditure authorisations, is the final step preceding execution of the project.

(B) Operating Phase: This phase involves implementation of the plan through generation of reports with the aid of sophisticated peripheral equipment, such as computer planning systems, and subsequent submittal, evaluation and feedback from the functional management.

*Techniques*

The mere intervention of managers in projects endeavours the application of necessary techniques that match the requirements of these projects, contingent upon the degrée of sophistication under pursuit. One key factor becomes the provision of reporting schemes, usually in the form of schedules, as a vehicle of effective and efficient communication. Such schedules have been adapted to the trends of the computer era, the most popularly renowned ones to be PERT. CPM, GANTT, MOST and LOB.

The objective of PERT (Programme Evaluation and Review Technique) is to provide planning and evaluation information at the proper levels, with the aid of an integrated management information system. The expected duration for each activity must be estimated and for this purpose three different types of time durations are computed: the most pessimistic, the most optimistic, and the most likely.

This process is necessary because most applications using PERT deal with research and development, where there is a great deal of uncertainty. Once all activity durations are estimated the networks total completion time can be calculated. Each event is numbered and each activity is presented showing the path necessary for completion of the project. The manager using PERT can evaluation alternatives by seeing how they can affect the overall completion date of the project.

An alternative network approach is the Critical Path Method (CPM). This method stresses emphasis on the monitoring of the critical path (refer to the glossary at Annexure I) in order to secure efficient completion of the project. Its implementation is subject to the availability or cost-time relationships data.

The major difference between PERT and CPM lies in the fact that PERT is the concept of uncertains for calculating activity duration, while CPM uses a single-calculated duration. CPM emphasises the relationship between applying more resources to shorten duration and the increased cost of the additional resources. The amount of time and additional resousces necessary to complete the project is assumed to be known as opposed to PERT which relies on uncertainty. For this reason CPM is frequently used in construction projects were situations portraying these features have been experienced. Both PERT and CPM are extensively used in planning and scheduling except for those industries engaged in small-scale projects and which require less sophisticated monitoring systems.

As part of its ventures, the Lycoming Division of AVCO Corporation, based in Strattford, Connecticut, USA, became concerned with the application of PERT technique. Although handy in nature, a proved costly when applied in the evaluation of small of medium used projects.

As view of this shortcoming, the group engaged in an effort to devise a system offering great flexibility, simplicity and inexpensiveness. Through combinations of features from traditional planning techniques, such as BAR, GANTT charts, PERT, etc., a system developed. This Management Operations System Technique (MOST) emerged.[5]

This system presents planning, scheduling and costing graphically in an easily readable chart or network. It can be employed in search, development, construction, and manufacturing projects. MOST, unlike PERT/CPM, is a graphical illustration of performance way and cost on a network pattern. MOST networks are drawn on such wide reproducible paper, and unlike PERT, they begin on the provide using contractual completion dates, and work backwards, is a bar chart technique.[6] Each job, as it is called, is represented by a 1/8 inch bar closed with flags at right angles to note its starting and ending points. When estimating job times, they can be recorded on the network using the bar at the bottom of the network.[7] It also identifies the critical path, which is the longest path on the network and is darkened, for illustration purposes. Both illustrate slack time, expected time (te), most likely time (tm), optimistic time (to), pessimistic time (ts), for the critical path.

The transition from PERT to MOST is not difficult. The planner does not have to be a draftsman, artist or mathematician to interpret it. He must have the ability to use people and details and to display the necessary elements on paper in their proper sequences. Note that MOST uses the tree approach in its network design. Like PERT, the MOST network is a fast, reliable and comprehensive feedback to aid in planning decisions. Among its advantages can be mentioned:

(1) It saves time in computations;

(2) Reduces manpower requirements in planning;

(3) Increases the utilisation of information;

(4) Because of its simplicity, it can be learned quickly; and

(5) Reduces size of planning charts.

**Cost Considerations in Project Management**

A third important phase in Project Management, besides planning and implementation, is that of costing.

The total cost of a programme is usually estimated through pricing of all the activities undertaken over the scheduled period of performance. All the functional units of the project team must partcipate in this task, and the central target of pricing becomes the Work Breakdown Structure. This task is one of a bottom-up type in the sense that costing information flows from the project level to the total programme level.

One major consideration is that of changing environmental conditions (such as fluctuations in raw materials and labour costs), which indeed affects cost estimates for projects under great uncertainty.

The basic components of a costing system in Project Management are materials/support costs, labour distribution costs and overheads. These components are reported on a periodical basis, as the project gets closer and closer to its completion. Regular comparison of actual incurrences *vs.* estimates based on some experiment history is ensured, so that provisions are made to account for this cost differential at the completion stage of the project.

Once the project cost is obtained, costing activities at a programme stage are undertaken by higher-level management. This is evidently a corporate-oriented engagement.

In conclusion, the structure of project management for the future will experience a new revitalisation, both in terms of applications and concepts. One can infer about the following future developments most likely to affect project management:

1. Project management concepts will become more disciplined and analytical;
2. Projects will be more complex, multi-faceted, and long-term in nature;
3. Project management techniques will become universally applied;
4. There will be increased interaction between project managers and traditional managers in organisations;
5. Better monitoring devices and techniques for planning, controlling and scheduling will be developed;
6. Computerisation of project management will affect both hardware and software type projects; and
7. Man-machine type products will surface in both private and public enterprises.

## REFERENCES


1. *Basis of Project Management*, AMA Seminar, New York, 1977, p. 1.
2. Martin, C., *Project Management: How to Make It Work*, New York, Amacon, 1976, p. 1.
3. *Basic Project Management*, AMA Seminar *op. cit.*
4. Killian, William P., "Project Management—Future Organisational Concepts," *Marqueue Business Review*, No. 2. 1971, pp. 90-107.
5. Iannone. A., *Management Programme Planning & Control with PERT, MOST. LOB*, New Jersey, Prentice-Hall, 1971.
6. *Ibid.*, p. 96.
7. *Ibid.*, p. 104.

## *ANNEXURE-I*

**Glossary**

*Activity.* The work necessary to proceed from one event to the next. Activities requiring time, manpower, facilities, or other resources are represented by arrows in a network diagram.

*Arrow.* A directed line, connecting two events, that depicts the activity necessary to move from the predecessor event to the successor event.

*Critical. Path* That particular sequence of events and activities in a path that has the least value slack; therefore, the longest path through the network.

*Detail Network.* A network which reflects activities lowest level of the programme breakdown.

*Duration.* The estimated completion time for an activity (task).

*Milestones.* They are synonymous with events in a network.

*Management Operation System Technique* (*MOST*). A management planning technique that uses a graphical illustration of performance time and cost on an easily read network.

*Network.* A flow-diagram depicting the activities and events which must be accomplished to reach the programme objectives; it shows their planned sequences of accomplishments, interdependencies, and interrelationships.

*Programme Evaluation and Review Technique* (*PERT*). A management planning tool that uses a graphic network, based on Work Breakdown Structure, to correctly sequence and relate interrelationship.

# 2

# PROJECT PREPARATION

We have seen that the project preparation phase is the first major stage of the plant investment process. First in sequence, it has profound implications for what follows; the project preparation stage sows the seeds of success, mischief or disaster.

The project preparation stage embraces all the activities between the moment of 'stimulus response' and the presentation of a definitive proposal for authorisation. The three main sub-sections of this stage consist of:

1. Feasibility analysis.
2. Authorisation of project development resources.
3. Project development and definition.

One can expect to find these stages for every project above a certain size (say, £250000 at 1978 prices) and also for many below such level. It will be noted from Figures 2.1-3 that each section can comprise quite a number of activities. Depending on the project, these need not all be carried out within the company. Management consultants, consulting engineers or, in some industries, prospective main contractors may participate in this work. Obviously, there will be many small projects where some of the indicated task components will not be needed. For instance, a straightforward, but minor, expansion project may require little more of the project preparation stage than proposal definition. All the basic information is already available and its collation requires little time and effort. However, a cost reduction project involving technical change may encompass all stages. In principle, the totality of the project preparation stage depends on the complexity of the evolving proposition.

### Feasibility Analysis

As we can see from Figure 2.1 the input to this part of the project preparation system consists of stimuli—ideas of all sorts.

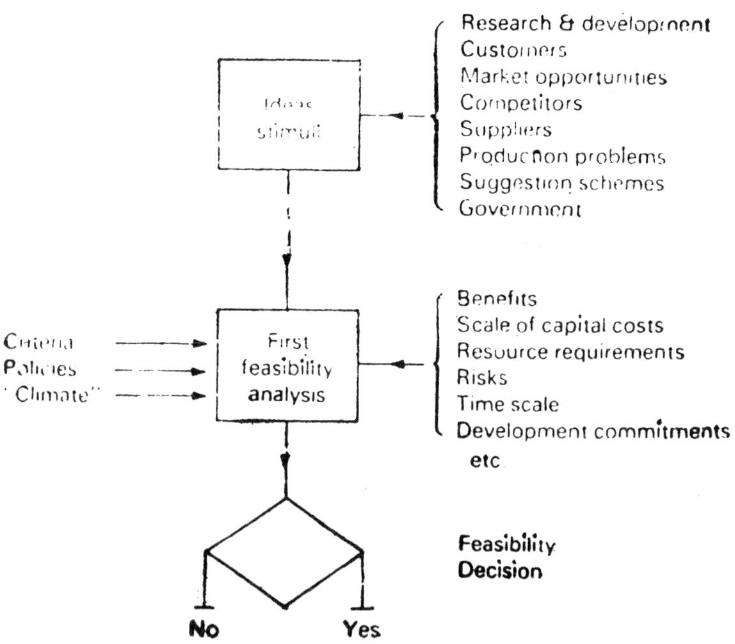


**Figure 2.1** The concept of feasibility analysis

They come from many quarters, both from within and outside the firm. They can be random or be at encouraged by management such as through suggestion schemes, brainstorming sessions, value analysis, lateral thinking and similar techniques. The catchment of stimuli, the establishment of ideas portfolios—this is the first opportunity within the investment process for an alert management. Needless to say, the 'climate' of the company, its organisational behaviour, governs the success of such intentions.

When a firm visualises an investment opportunity in new production plant we imply an opportunity awareness at an appropriate decision-making level. This is either at a level of authority at which decisions about commensurate company resources can be made or, alternatively, at an immediately subordinate level whose proposals are normally given serious consideration by the first group. Such an interpretation will therefore rule out the investment idea or opportunity awareness, however promising, which is possessed by an employee, who is at a level substantially below the appropriate decision level in the company hierarchy. Only when the ideas reach such a level can they be considered. This may be significant in the context of a firm's information system; whatever stimulus reaches the decision-making level, whether by intent or chance, is likely to obtain speedier attention than the stimuli which first have to be absorbed and transcribed by such a system.

Let us now presume that the opportunity is perceived at the appropriate level—what happens ? Perception is a mental recognition by one or more individuals of the existence and suggested implications of an opportunity. The implications need to be meaningful to those concerned in terms of criteria by which their affairs are judged. Such implications may be expressed in terms of profit, sales, productivity, quality, etc., and possibly a whole host of other considerations which seem relevant to those involved. The opportunity may be described in a crude form of proposition which embodies the insight or reflection following perception. The proposition is crude in the sense that no organisational resources have been applied to its definition or validation. (This excludes the possibility that a particular executive espouses an idea and develops it without the knowledge of his organisation.)

Essentially, feasibility analysis is the first inspection of an incipient proposition. It endeavours to establish: (i) the merits of the proposition in terms of the chosen criteia, (ii) the costs expected to be incurred; (iii) the company resources required, and (iv) the likely risks involved. The purpose of this first view is to establish whether the envisaged opportunity should have formal recognition within the organisation. If the proposition is given such a status then resources, if needed, can be allocated to it for its further development. Such recognition is in practice often given by the issue of a project number or accounts code. Feasibility analysis does not confirm the ultimate worth or promise of a proposition. All it does is to decide which propositions are worth some organisational support for further consideration; or where the inverse is more important, which proposals to leave alone. Where so much is tentative the judgements are largely subjective even on relatively technical matters. The nature of the organisational framework and the climate of expectations are important and it is here that well-thoughtout policies provide a helpful setting for the first stage of decision making.

The initial feasibility study is usually, but not necessarily, carried out by the functional department which responded to the original stimulus. Informal discussions with other interested department may, of course, be included in this. For instance, a growing factory work load may prompt a production manager to consider a plant extension. Initial discussions with marketing would seek to establish the permanence of current market trends. There is some expectation by the initiating department that it would have operational control of the proposed capital equipment. This would not happen in every case, but where feasibility is confirmed, a chaperon for the proposition usually emerges and it is appropriate that it should be those concerned with the operational realisation of the proposal.

The actual mechanics of a first appraisal are often informal, such as the 'back of the envelope' calculation. It is, however, relatively easy to put feasibility analysis on a systematic basis. An idea usually has an exponent or sponsor. He can enter on a simple form a description of the idea, its purpose, prospects and problems. To the first analysis can also be added a 'second opinion'—someone sufficiently apart from the proposal to have no prior views could act as an auditor. This is particularly valuable where a plant proposition has a significant development/design content. This type of approach is common with suggestion schemes and can be applied to other situations.

The marshalling and tentative evaluation of all relevant data provides the setting for the feasibility decision. The main proposition elements (capital costs, revenue benefits, risks and implications) are related to given criteria and policies. The decision often combines economic and technical judgement. The decision may be made by the functional manager concerned or sometimes by a technical committee responsible for such first-stage decisions.

It the proposal has survived this first hurdle, it will pass to the next section of the preparation system.

**The Authorisation of Project Resources**

The proposal, designated as 'feasible', enters the next struggle for survival. It is now formally recognised and quickly becomes a claimant of resources. Subsequent growth and success is a function of the resources it will be able to obtain. In this respect, proposal needs are variable and have to be matched with what can be supplied. Our 'infant' project is usually in competition with other claimants.

The resources consists primarily of managerial and technical staff capable of developing, shaping and refining a capital expenditure proposition. Of course, other resources are also needed; for instance, in a process or plant development situation these could, typically, include equipment and meterials.

However, the quantity and quality of the available specialist resources remain the key to progress at this stage. These resources can be augmented; additional staff can be recruited and trained. But there is a limit to this, particularly in the short run. The supply of some specialists is relatively inelastic and the time-lag before a firm receives an effective contribution from such extra staff can be considerable. Also, management may be hesitant about violent swings in such staff resources. Alternatives, such as the contracting-out of certain preparation tasks, typically routine draughting work, may be possible to a limited extent. Similarly, the technical staff of a consultant or a would be contractor may be used. The need, however, for such additional resources is greatest where the project has a large development content—and these are the very cases where outside assistance is less suitable.

The main constituents of the project resources authorisation process are shown in Figure 2.2. These presume the more complex project situation where the scale, mix and technical content of the prospective project call for systematic difinition and computation of manpower requirements. Typically, this is a large composite project with a strong design development content. It must be remembered that only project preparation resources are involved. Where the scale and complexity of a project are more modest, informal, short-cut methods will be common. Nevertheless, in principle, these stages occur, even if they are reduced to an intuitive level.

Proposal feasibility can be taken to mean that on first view the proposal holds sufficient promise to warrant further development. In essence, there is a basic credibility about the idea. However, there is no certainty about its success. One of the tasks of project preparation is to study the implications of the proposal, particularly the major problems. Preparation work is as much risk reduction as proposition crystallisation.

*Proposal resources definition.* Resources definition for project preparation is, then, primarily concerned with the manpower requirements to generate a meaningful investment

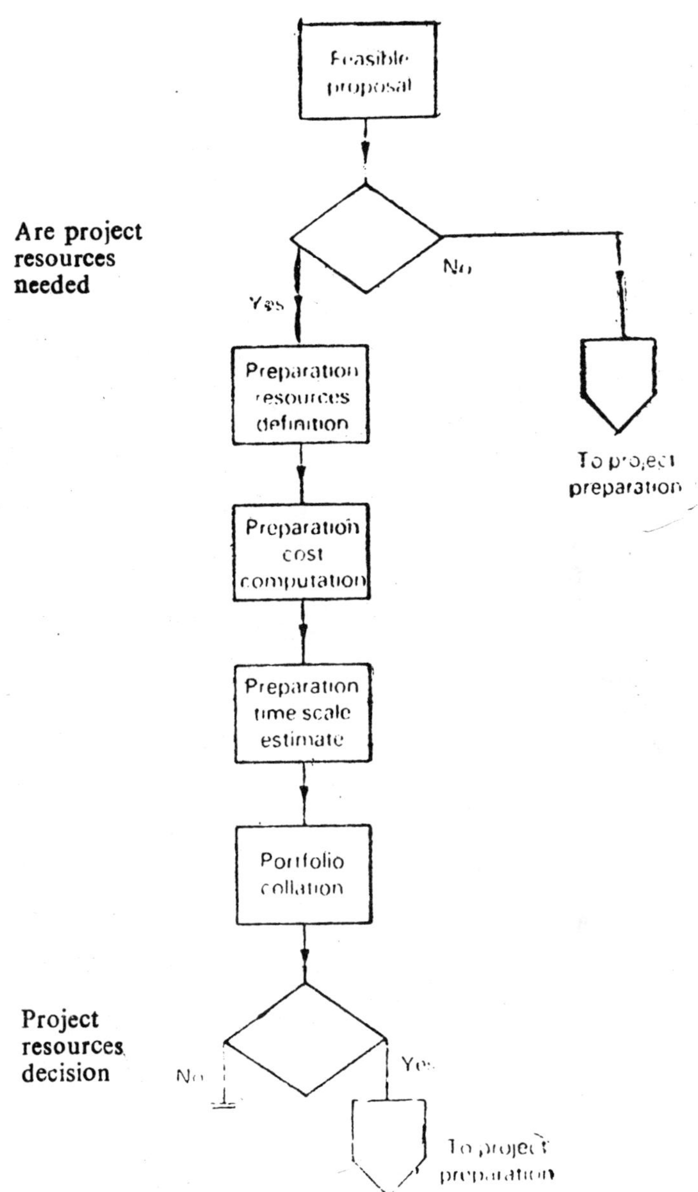


**Figure 2.2** Authorisation of project preparation resources

proposition. Taking an example, this might read: thirty men/month for mechanical design, ten men/month for model prototype work, etc., etc. A measure of prospective staff loading would thus be obtained. Such a preliminary assessment is similar to the process of shop loading in a production department where the capacity requirements of a particular job have to be established for scheduling and machine allocation purposes. Indeed, with the growing costs and problems of hiring staff and subsequently declaring them redundant—only to need them again, say, six months later—certain groups of key technologists may acquire some of the characteristics of 'fixed assets' calling for much more systematic work estimating and planning to ensure economic operations.

*Preparation cost computation.* Once basic resource requirements have been estimated these can be transcribed into costs. Staff time requirements multiplied by the appropriate cost rates furnish the initial manpower costs. To these have to be added supporting project expenses such as materials. The basis of computation and the allocation of overheads depend, of course, on the system of management accounting operated by the firm. Whatever that might be in detail, it should clearly delineate the incremental cost of a particular proposal development.

It must be remembered that the costs of proposal development are generally incorporated in the plant investment submission. The expenditure, so to speak, is on account, in the hope and expectation of project success If this yields effective production plant the expense may be capitalised retrospectively. (Taxation aspects need to be examined separately.) If the proposal development gets difficulties or the subsequent capital expenditure request is not authorised, the expense incurred up to that date will have to be written off if sizeable or absorbed, by a general development account. It is presumed here that proposal development work is separately recorded and costed. Where costs are likely to be small they may be absorbed within departmental budgets.

*Time scale definition.* It is now possible to furnish a preparation resources and cost estimate together with a time scale for proposal submission. This is input information for the scheduling of technical manpower and for the resources authorisation decision. The time scale can also be significant for development cost cash-flow reasons. It further indicates when the main investment decision can be taken. In a competitive situation the timing of that decision could be important.

*Proposal portfolio collation.* With a substantial company a number of feasible proposals can emerge in a given period. Within an established system they are all subject to the same evaluation process. Now they are assembled for project resources authorisation. Collation here is more than mere listing because of possible proposal interaetion effects. The periodic portfolio decision approach gives a better overview and facilitates the integration of subsequent investment proposal development. Alternatively, decisions can be made on individual proposals as they emerge.

*The resources authorisation decisions.* As already indicated, the resources authorisation decision is concerned with those composite plant investment opportunities which make substantial calls on preporatory resources. It settles to which opportunities the available resources shall be applied. Calls are matched with available or prospective resources and ongoing commitments. Proposals which require none or so little that they can be accommodated by the 'organisational slack' (extra built-in work capacity) bypass the whole of this module and proceed to the preparation task. The decision process becomes similar to those used for selecting research and development projects. These have been well documented by Beattie and Reader.[1] Some of the economic decision aspects will be discussed in the next section. At this stage it should be remembered that projects can be considered individually or in clusters, that schedules may be specified for the supported projects and that a 'no' may only be until the next review period. Policy considerations, such as the use of 'know-how' and technical exchange agreements with other firms, can also be important considerations here.

The decisions are often made by formal or informal technical or management committees chaired or guided by a board member particularly concerned with corporate plans.

**Project Development and Definition**

We come now to the core of the project preparation process. It will be seen from Figure 2.3 that this consists of four modules: Preparation planning, Detailed functional analysis, Functional development and Proposal definition. This is the full model which incorporates the special aspects of an investment proposal associated with development and technical change. Again, for simpler cases the modules will be reduced in number and content.

*Preparation Planning*

The preparation planning stage applies where the project preparation task is substantial and/or complex. The nature of the operation requires definition of what is to be done, by whom and by what date. Preparation planning is comparable in structure to project planning. The difference is in the objectives. The latter is normally concerned with tangible results—typically, new machines; processes or buildings—here, the end product is a document, a proposition. Yet the proposition, to be credible, has to anticipate and simulate these physical developments.

The first task is a more detailed specification of intent. To some extent this may already have been anticipated at the feasibility analysis and resources authorisation stages. The basic terms of reference may already be there. For example, these could be: prepare within six months the specification and estimate for a new factory in Brazil, given the choice of three alternative capacity levels or product mixes. Or, submit within

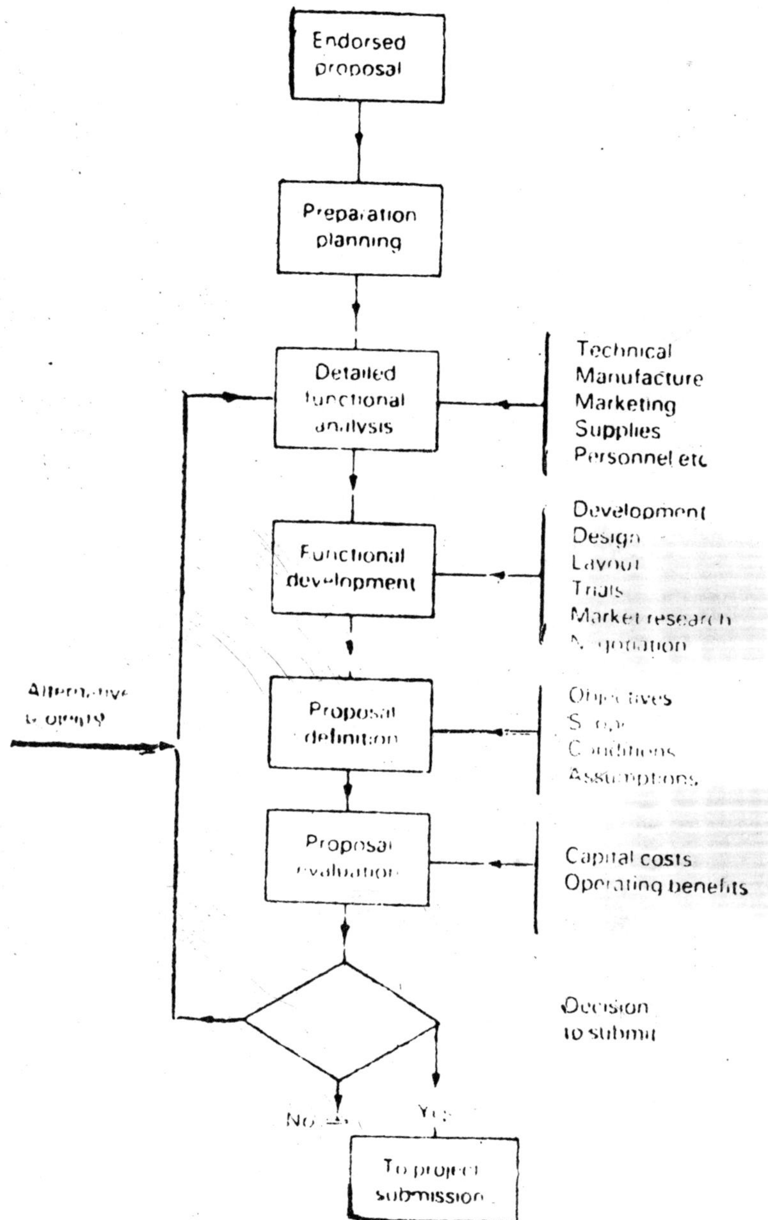


**Figure 2.3** The structure of project preparation

three months fully costed and documented proposals for a machine line running at three very different alternative speeds. The more detailed statement of intent is designed to furnish a basis for action. To this end it develops the outline of the project preparation stage; it gives structure to the work to come. The statement of intent is usually circulated to all specialist sections which are expected to contribute to the project formulation.

This first task is commonly carried out by a 'project manager.' The individual who has been given this responsibility may specialise in project management. This often happens with large companies in the process industries where the continuity of work permits such division of labour. Alternatively, it could be anyone, seconded on a full-time basis or merely charged with an extra duty, who has the responsibility for this specific task. This person may or may not have the status of manager in the wider context of company organisation. The selection and manner of appointment of such a manager is of course a vital part of the preparation planning phase. Much of what will happen as the project develops can be ascribed, for better or for worse, to this particular step. Of course, the selected individual may already have been associated with the previous feasibility analysis.

Next, the project manager, or, if the scale of operation warrants it, his staff, then prepares a timetable for the various stages of project preparation. This includes the definition of the main task constituents. Much of the work here is the coordination of specialist activities, and the timetable has to integrate their respective contributions in a manner which is economic, technologically feasible and consistent with the overall target time. The development of such a programme requires the solution of scheduling and resources problems. For complex situations an elaborate activity network may have to be developed.

In large companies a standard practice for the required organisation and coordination often already exists. Otherwise the framework of coordination has to be developed and this framework has to encompass the different activities of functional analysis and subsequent proposal definition. This is particularly important where the firm is about to embark on a venture which dwarfs what is considered to be the normal project. The accepted organisational assumptions no longer hold when the project is, say, ten times the usual scale.

It is axiomatic that as part of the project organisational development the project manager will be responsible for the definition of the communication system between the project participants, the reporting procedures to top management (where not already defined) and the manner of staff cost control.

*Functional Analysis*

This stage of the preparation process begins when those concerned have received the instructions and guidance they require to carry out their specialist tasks. Not all the specialists can start at once—their entry is determined by the logic of the technology involved. For instance, with a large process plant the electrical engineer can only specify a motor when the mechanical engineer has determined what pump should be used; in turn, the latter waits until the chemical engineer has determined the material flow conditions.

But whatever the timing of their entry, they will be concerned with the analysis of the project brief in the context of their specialisation. They assess the meaning and the feasibility of that brief, the problems it generates and the constraints within which a solution needs to be found. A series of investigations may be called for or outside consultants may need to be retained. A typical illustration is the drilling of test holes for the foundations of a new factory. Without knowledge of the load-bearing soil characteristics it would be impossible to determine the nature or cost of such foundations. The structural stability of the newly-built factory could be affected and thus introduce a special risk. We can thus view the purpose of functional analysis to be the ascertainment of the nature and degree of risk associated with each facet of the project proposal. The investigations and enquiries are designed to eliminate the risks, or at least to reduce them to acceptable proportions. This depends on the ability to control the factors involved. A technical production problem may be fully resolved in a 'controlled' situation; a marketing problem may be hostage to the strategies of others.

Two specific aspects can affects the functional analysis. Firstly, some of the relevant work may have already been carried out at the feasibility analysis stage, *i.e.*, a key problem was anticipated and, in substance, has already been resolved. Secondly, the firm may have established standard practices to which some of investigations have to conform. For example, a firm may require its design staff to carry out very specific calculations as to the size and costs of process pipelines. In such cases the structure of the investigation is determined by calculation sheets, specification forms and computer packages.

Figure 2.3 lists the more important functional areas of the firm with which analysis will be concerned, namely technology, manufacture, marketing, supplies, personnel. The list is not exclusive; special sitautions sould exist, for instance, where key aspects of investigation focus on the validity of a patent or the feasibility of a licensing agreement. A straight expansion project might emphasise markets, supplies and human resources as the main subject for investigation. A cost reduction project pays more attention to engineering, plant and process matters.

An important aspect of project management is to spot and to classify all significant problems which the analysis encounters. Some can be contained within their specialist categories; others have wider repercussions. For instance, in the manufacture of antibiotics the problem of bacteriological contamination affects many aspect of process and plant analysis. Again some problems may be resolved, within the specified time by a crash programme of staff concentration. Others, more intractable, may be insoluble within the period of the project preparation horizon. The project intent may have to be restated in order to bypass the problem. Failing that, the project could be in jeopardy. Even the early recognition of this has its merits.

The anticipation, or at least the prompt detection, of problems is part of effective project management; it helps to contain both delay and costs. The onus remains on the project manager to ensure that the magnitude of the problem is matched by corresponding resources. As he is essentially a coordinator—he usually has no line authority over specialist contributors—much will depend on his skills of coordination and communication. (The latter applies both laterallv and vertically upwards.)

### *Functional Development*

Functional development is a close follower of functional analysis. In practice, the boundary can be quite fuzzy. Analytically speaking, the two can be distinguished as follows: one is concerned with the assessment and resolution of relevant problems, the other is a synthesis of findings. Constituents of the proposal begin to take shape. In the production situation, development means the definition of particular items of plant or, at a more integrated level, the disposition of such plant in a new factory layout. Where technical change is involved it includes the development and design of new plant in the engineering sense. In special cases it can also involve the building and testing of prototype units; we are here at the borderline between development work in the conventional sense and investment preparation. With a marketing or commercial content there could be test marketing and a range of exploratory negotiations.

The investment proposal is not yet defined but some important constituents, around which the proposal mix will be built, are beginning to crystallise. The main criterion at this stage is operational feasibility. Technological feasibility is, of course, a fundamental part of this. Economic feasibility considerations are implied rather than explicit at this stage although an obviously basic cost factor is bound to get attention. However, this is more likely to form part of 'good' design or engineering practice rather than as a component of project evaluation.

With a large technical project content, functional development can be an expensive and time-consuming process. Here the emphasis is on the cost control aspect of project management. Everything is tentative in a financial sense; there is no guarantee that the subsequent capital expenditure submission will be authorised. The problem is the location of the cut-off point. The work should be sufficiently advanced to give confidence in its eventual success, yet without incurring unnecessary losses, should the project have to be stopped.

### *Proposal Definition*

This is a more familiar part of the project preparation stage. It is found with every meaningful investment proposal, whereas some of the other modules may not necessarily occur. It takes the different contributions from the development stage and integrates them into one or several propositions. An overall picture emerges. Integration includes here the elimination of inconsistencies or gaps between the specialist contributions.

The defined proposal will be in document form. Its main constituents will be the following:

*A statement of objectives.* Typically, this could be a statement of output or an increase in production. Alternatively, it might be a statement of product quality or cost reduction. Again, the project objective could be the attainment of a particular step within a broader strategy.

*The method of achievement.* This is a description as to how the objectives are to be attained. Under this heading would be specified new processes or production methods, *i.e.*, the general outline of the proposed facilities as seen in the context of a given operational situation.

*Listing of proposed plant and buildings.* This is largely an inventory of the main project constituents. Key plant details which justify operational selection may also be given. Some boards prefer to see the full technical or suppliers' specifications of major plant items. In these case they usually appear as appendices in the proposal brochure. Similarly, with new buildings or factory sites, architectural schemes and basic layouts are enclosed. In general, the narrative content depends on the complexity of the proposal as well as its organisational environment.

*The estimate of capital expenditure.* This is a statement of the expected capital cost of the proposal. The total may be expressed as a single value or as a range of figures. With larger projects the overall value is usully broken down into subtotals for key sections within a framework of accounting codes. In a different manner the totoal may also be expressed in a cash-flow form, showing typically the pattern for equipment deposit and delivery payments. This also applies to progress payments for construction work. Many firms make it a practice to append to the estimate notes as to their accuracy classification and to specify the key assumptions on which the calculations are based. Similarly, contingency requirements are listed, typically, to allow for escalation.

*The benefit statement.* Where the project is justified on economic grounds the statement will describe the expected net revenue gain due to the proposed capital expenditure. The gain may be due to the extra contribution from sales, either as a result of increased volume or margins. Alternatively, it can be due to cost reduction and, of course, a mixture of the two main sources is also possible. These benefits may be shown for a year,, with the implied assumption—not always tenable—of their continuity; or they are projected over a specified horizon, say, five years. The benefit need not be expressed in quantified economic terms; a safety or welfare argument could be marshalled in its place.

*The time scale.* A project or, for that matter, any venture without a time scale has no real meaning. The two relevant measures incorporated in the project definition are the duration of the project itself, *i.e.*, the time span during which resources are expended on capital account and the expected life span of the plant in question.

These are the major parts of the proposal and the absence of any one could significantly weaken it. This does not however require complete enumeration every time in a document form. For instance, with routine and relatively minor plant replacement projects some of these statements may be subsumed within established manufacturing policies. But the more important the project, the stronger is the case for an explicit statement in the proposal.

A number of additional features are often found depending on the systems operated by a particular management. Some firms couple the project evaluation with the proposal definition stage. This may reflect organisational philosophy or the commonsense argument that those who prepare the proposal should see for themselves whether it makes economic sense. At the risk of being arbitrary we shall discuss investment evaluation in the next chapter. Before embarking on this, however, there are some observations to be made on the industrial practice of project definition.

## *Some Observations on Proposal Definition*

It is useful to recall the section commencing on page 29 and the large number of capital expenditure applications that need to be processed by any firm of size. Standard presentation helps appraisal and decision, particularly where, as in a portfolio situation, project proposals need to be compared and ranked. Yet such presentation may still conceal differences in interpretation, computation and assumptions, all of which could affect the judgement of the decision makers. This has prompted top management to consider in some detail the whole process of proposal definition. The result is the operating manual or administrative procedure which establishes the principles and detail practice of proposal definition. Proposal definition is usually the substance of the first chapter; subsequent to this come appropriate instructions on the evaluation, presentation and authorisation mechanism of projects.

Three out of four of the associated companies operated such a system. The fourth used five-year forecasts for the planning of expansion in manufacturing capacity. The systems emphasis was on the annual capital expenditure budget for every department and factory rather than on the individual proposal.

All companies had standard capital expenditure application forms. These contained interesting variations in purpose and complexity. The procedure adopted by companies A and B were applicable both to capital expenditure and special revenue expenditure proposals. Companies C and D confined their system to the former. To this purpose their operating instructions defined the term capital expenditure for guidance in project preparation. Company C interpreted it as follows:

> 'For the purpose of this procedure, Capital Expenditure represents the acquisition of a permanent asset whose value exceeds £50 which has a life of not less than one year and is not usually expended in the normal course of production. It also includes office furniture and equipment whose value exceeds £25. . .In addition all expenses directly related to the acquisition of these assets shall be included as part of the amounts involved when submitting a request for Capital Expenditure (*e.g.*, installation, freight, duty, rearrangement, dismantling or removal costs). . .'

Company D employed the following definition:

'Capital expenditure is defined as:

1.1 Any expenditure that increase, or improves the fixed assets of the business, together with *and* for the purpose *only* of calculating per cent return:

1.2 Any increase in the net working capital of the business to finance a project. For this purpose net working capital is defined as stock plus debtors less creditors'.

The capital expenditure application was the embodiment of the project proposal. It was essentially a multi-page document. With company A this consisted of a project description, financial summary, details of investment cash needed, cash details of benefit and a cash-flow graph. The company C system incorporated a project summary, cost analysis, machinery and building detail sheets. Company D had a basic capital project form, supported by an evaluation summary, plant list and working capital statement. Apart from these basic documents it had specialist forms for market forecasts, labour cost savings, ingredient savings—to be used by the proposers as required.

The detailed form design reflected each company's manner of project proposal definition. It was rather affected by the prescribed method of project evaluation. It showed what top management regarded as important in a commercial sense, with explicit computation steps for key data. Periodic updating of the forms allowed for systems changes and the effect of government measures relating to investments.

All forms required a statement of justification for the proposed scheme. The justification could be a specific and newly-established expectation or a reference to an already agreed and documented decision. In some cases the proposer had to select a justification category, *e.g.*, in company B he had to choose from the following defined and illustrated classification:

'Company Reorganisation
Diversification into New Products
Expansion of Capacity for Existing Lines
Others

Profit Improvement Projects
Quality, Hygiene, Welfare and Amenity
Replacements
Safety, Security and Statutory Requirements.'

The relationship between a particular proposal and the general capital expenditure budget seemed to get only a partial acknowledgement in the documents. Only companies C and D required the proposer to refer to a budget allocation, if any. This does, however, suggest an interesting two-stage mechanism. The first stage is the inclusion, without promise, of a particular proposal in the capital expenditure budget. (We are referring here to the type of project which can normally be financed by the company's depreciation cashflow). The second stage is the actual evaluation in the conventional sense, which determines the fate of the proposal. The first stage indicates a periodic 'draft' dialogue between project proposers (or sponsors at departmental management level) and the investment decision makers.

The administrative instructions gave considerable attention to the 'form-filling' parts of the proposal. Guidance and illustrations were commonly given to ensure that the forms would be used consistently and universally. This included, for instance, instructions on graph preparation by company A. Company D used flow diagrams to explain to users some of the key aspects of preparation and work coordination. Other interesting features of instructions were requirements as to the discussion of risks, an account of feasible alternatives, considered but not submitted, and comparisons with competitors.

The manner of yield calculation was made very explicit by company A to ensure that all staff concerned understood its particular pattern. This reflected its policy that those who prepared a proposal should be the first to evaluate it. However, it did not specify a set rate of return. Only company C gave such instructions: its staff had to assess projects on a 15 per cent DCF present-value basis.

The urgency level of some projects was recognised by company C. It had a procedure for 'emergency requests' in the case of fire, damage caused by the elements, unexpected breakdowns in production, etc. The personnel concerned had to decide whether to use the standard procedure or to seek verbal approval which was confirmed by an emergency release form. This is an interesting reminder of operational conditions in a capital-intensive process industry.

All systems had definite rules as to who was responsible for form completion. Provisions were made on the capital request summary form for the signatures of the originators, verifying specialists and appropriate operational managers. Company D had an explicit responsibility chart for this. A simplified version of this is shown in Figure 2.4.

**Check List: Project Preparation**

*Basic*

1. Does our company have a standard practice and forms for the preparation and submission of capital expenditure projects?
2. Who is responsible for the maintenance and updating of specified procedures?
3. When were they last reviewed? Does each form have a date and a revision number?
4. Who should have a copy of the procedures?
5. Are the procedures well integrated with other standard practices? Any gaps or overlaps?

*Feasibility*

1. What happens to good project ideas in our company?
2. Think of a good project idea which was not developed. Why did it not survive?
3. What is our catchment system for ideas?

| *Responsibiliiy for completion* ———→<br><br>CAPITAL PROJECT FORM | Originator | Evaluating Accountant | Factory Director | Divisional Controller | Group Finance | Group Production Services Director |
|---|---|---|---|---|---|---|
| Project number | | | | x | x | |
| Location | x | | | | | |
| Description of project | x | | | | | |
| Estimated commissioning date | x | | | | | |
| Estimated life of asset | x | | | | | |
| Asset classification | x | | | | | |
| Cost figures | x | | | | | |
| Working capital | | x | | | | |
| Budget details | x | | | | | |
| Justification category | x | | | | | |
| Aditional justification | x | | | | | |
| Predicted performance | | x | | | | |
| Signatures—Originator | x | | | | | |
| —Reviewing function | | | | | | x |
| —Evaluating Accountant | | x | | | | |
| —Reviewing Accountant | | | x | x | | |
| Approved/rejected | | x | x | x | x | |
| *Appendices* | | | | | | |
| Evaluating summary | | x | | | | |
| Summary (main points) | | x | | | | |
| Analysis and detail of gross cost | x | | | | | |

Figure 2.4 Example of project verification responsibility chart

4. What techniques do you use for generating ideas? Brainstorming? Lateral thinking? Value analysis?
5. Do we have a suggestion scheme? Can its contribution be increased?
6. Are there simple guidelines for feasibility analysis?
7. Design a simple form for idea feasibility assessment.
8. How would you retrieve such an idea in two years' time?

*Plant Definition*

1. What are the operational requirements?
   (a) Volume/rate of output.
   (b) Quality.
   (c) Equipment Reliability.
   (d) Safety.
   (e) Operating Costs.
   (f) Manning.
   (g) Efficiencies.
2. Who will be affected by these requirements? Have they been told verbally, in writing?
3. What are the implications of these requirements on:
   (a) Other plant.
   (b) Buildings.
   (c) Services (including effluents).
   (d) Storage facilities.
   (e) Material handling.
   (f) Roads, access, gangways?

4. What will be the effects on industrial relations?
   (a) Changes in techniques.
   (b) Staff transfers.
   (c) Redundancies.
   (d) New skills, re-grading.
   (e) Recruitment, training.

*Purchased Equipment*

1. Have you satisfied yourself as to the supplier's capacity and reputation? (Vendor analysis)

2. Does the proposed equipment meet your requirements? If it falls short in some respects, what will be the operational implications and costs?

3. Is the offered equipment
   (a) Really proven?
   (b) About to become obsolescent?

4. Does the quoted price cover such costs as:
   (a) Transport.
   (b) Custom duties.
   (c) Insurances.
   (d) Installation and other site costs.
   (e) Commissioning.
   (f) Operator training.
   (g) Packaging.
   (h) Key spares?

5. How reliable is delivery? What would be the costs to you of a delay of 1,3,6 months?

6. What would be the life-cycle costs?

   (a) Operational: labour, material, services.

   (b) Maintenance: labour, material, spare inventory costs.

   (c) Downtimes due to breakdowns or malfunction.

7. What backup can you expect from the supplier?

   (a) Guarantees.

   (b) Service.

   (c) Instruction manuals.

   (d) Parts lists, spares.

   (e) Special tools and test equipment.

*Newly-developed Plant*

1. Have you the design, engineering and manufacturing resources?

2. How are staff resources costed and budgeted?

3. Have your staff sufficient relevant experience?

4. Has a prototype unit been developed? By you? By others?

5. Has the prototype plant been adequately tested on production runs?

6. If you are scaling up from a model or a pilot plant, what problems can be expected at full scale?

7. What will be the development costs from the prototype stage? Right from the beginning?

8. Many development projects ouerrun their budget. What would be the consequences if development costs were 50 per cent, 100 per cent, 200 per cent higher?

9. Could the development work be contracted out? At what cost?

10. How long will the development project take?

11. Are there side benefits with the developed plant, such as equipment sales to third parties?

12. Will you need specialist suppliers for parts and sub-systems?

13. Could there be patent complications?

*Proposal Definition*

1. Has the plant been fully specified and listed?

2. Is there a proper statement of the basis of design or operating principles for the new equipment?

3. Are key plant and layout drawings available?

4. What assumptions need to be listed about inputs, efficiencies and output levels?

5. What will be the expected plant life?

6. Will any existing plant be replaced? How will it be disposed of? Will there be residual cash flows?

7. How long will the project take to implement if authorised?

8. Have you obtained the full capital cost of equipment installed and connected up?

9. Have you included the provision of plant services (if any), site and building work?

10. Will there be royalty or know-how payments?

11. Are there any special revenue costs to be allowed for?

12. What project management and engineering charges have to be included?

13. Is working capital needed?

## REFERENCE

1. Beattie, C.J. and Reader, R.D., *Quantitative Management in R & D.* Chapman and Hall (London, 1971).

# 3

# PROJECT PRESENTATION AND AUTHORISATION

The brief is ready! The project is defined, documented, justified and evaluated; often it has travelled far. It has survived doubts, conflicts, the tugs of organisational war—now it waits in the ante-room of the decision makers. An interesting account of behavioural aspects of project presentation is given by Hopwood.[1]

This chapter is primarily concerned with how it makes its entry and what happens on arrival. We are interested in the presentation process so far as this reflects administrative practice within the total investment system. Similarly, we wish to look at some aspects of the decision process, known as project authorisation. In analysis the two process are, of course, quite distinct; in practice they can be very close.

## Project Presentation

The reader will recall that in Figure 2.3. 'The structure of project preparation' the overall investment system included the specific decision to present the proposal for authorisation. It might have seemed self-evident for the project sponsors to have taken their chance and automatically submitted their proposal in the belief that it was for top management to make the final decision. A project might look marginal or worse in a quantitative sense, yet have other arguments in its favour. Not only is it a matter here of delegating upwards, but the information environment at board level might provide better overall judgement. Indeed, the proposal itself has an information function, quite apart from the decision aspects. It can be a form of reporting of briefing on issues close to the interests of top management—we have then, in essence, the 'proforma' proposal. On the other hand, if a case lacked real merit, the sponsor's reputation would be at risk, although one could have expected such projects to have been filtered out at an earlier stage. Much, of course, depends here on the relationship between the decision makers and the project patrons.

There are cases where the authorisation process is in part anticipated by the presentation decision. A board may instruct its management or evaluating accountants not to present projects which are to be justified on economic grounds unless the yield is, say, 15 per cent. In that respect the presentation decision becomes a specific type of filter.

*The Mechanics of Presentation*

A further look at the mechanics of presentation is justified here. What, in the first instance, is meant by presentation and who makes it? Are there defined routes and do these vary with the size or source of the proposal? Presentation here means the formulated request for capital resources by someone entitled to ask for them and addressed to those who can authorise them. Depending on the project value, presentation therefore will be from the organisational level immediately below the authorisation level, *e.g.*, from the production manager to the factory manager, or from the managing director to his board. A project can thus climb several levels of the organisational hierarchy before being presented. It could fall at such intervening levels if support were withheld, yet it could not be authorised then. This is the process of endorsement, not authorisation.

Three of the four companies studied in detail defined the presentation routes in their instruction manuals. Thus, company A required all submissions to be made by a certain level of manager to the assistant managing director. In a similar vein, company C specified submission, in the first instance, to the group production director of all factory projects over £1000. The functional project source affected its route. So did size. The route was shorter for smaller projects where the amounts were within the discretion of intermediate levels of management The route was frequently defined by the format of the capital expenditure application form.

The formal route was thus defined; the speed along it was hostage to other considerations. Much depends on the attitude of certain members of the authorisation group, typically, the full-time director within whose functional area of control the project proposal was developed. If he was personally identified with the project and keen to see it to fruition he was likely to assist with the presentation task.

Apart from the presentation route, procedures generally were defined in some detail. In companies B, C and D it was the task of management accountants to ensure that procedures were followed. With the last two companies. instructions were specific and detailed, such as the obtaining of signatures, verification of form completeness, the issue of reference numbers, entry on application registers, etc.

A significant part of the presentation procedure related to the timetable of submission. For all projects of substance the timetable of submission was governed by the calendar of board meetings. For instance, with company D all projects to be considered by the board had to be received by the group management accountant at least ten days before the appropriate meeting. Of course, some very large projects might warrant special meetings. But apart from these, the flow of project proposals had a certain unevenness with minor peaks of project presentation when sponsors were anxious to catch a particular board meeting. The beginning of the annual budget period was particularly busy as projects were brought forward for sanction. Minor items such as office furniture were generally submitted at regular intervals, say quarterly, for collective authorisation.

All but a few projects were submitted in accordance with the specified procedures. Special situations did at times arise and in such case the system was short circuited. This occurred with plant emergencies (although that was also covered by procedures in company C) and special commercial situations—such as the obtaining of significant concessions or discounts on immediate plant orders. In these cases the decisions were confirmed by subsequent systems actuation. The commercial opportunities were more in the nature of timing than content; the intent had largely been formulated when external developments clinched the matter.

*The Capital Expenditure Request Document*

The analysis of the capital expenditure request documents of a number of companies indicates that the precise format and content reflect company systems which in turn are a function of the company's business. For instance, tooling costs are sufficiently frequent in the engineering industry to be a printed heading with some companies. A food company gives similar attention to ingredient savings. The design of appropriate forms is therefore a bespoke business. Documents have to reflect the needs of decision makers—this is basic to the design of any information and decision system. Nevertheless, the capital investment decision process has a set of principles which are independent of context and these must be acknowledged in detailed form design. While there is no ideal form which fits every company it is still possible to list the basic features of a good set of documents.

This section is concerned with the core of the submission document. The reader can relate his company situation to this core and add such other material as may be necessary. It is appreciated that small, routine projects would not need extensive documentation. Companies often have different documents for projects above or below specified values. For small projects the questioning on the form is simplified but there is no different of principle.

## The Capital Project Document

### *Form Design*

The two main considerations here are:

(i) the mechanics of form filling;

(ii) the process of information assimilation and decision making.

Form design was originally part of organisation and methods work (O & M) but has increasingly become the task of the systems analyst. This development is mainly due to two factors. The first is the growing use of computer-based systems. 'Why not let the computer do the form filling as well as the calculations?' The second is the role of the project form(s) for related purposes, such as project cash control or management information summaries.

The main features to be considered are:

1. The size and shape of forms.
2. The number of copies, their colour and distribution.
3. The title and the reference number of the form.
4. The numbering of forms or projects.
5. The pre-printing of standard or recurring items.
6. The structuring of the form layout to correspond to the logic of analysis.
7. Subsequent binding or filing.

*The Main Operational Constituents*

1. The title and reference number of the project.
2. A brief description of the purpose, scope and operational gains from the project.
3. A project expenditure summary comprising fixed assets, working capital and revenue expenses.
4. Project capital receipts; expected grants and realisations.
5. Project tax allowances.
6. Net project capital cost.
7. Capital expenditure cash flow distribution.
8. Project location: division, factory.
9. Asset categories: land, buildings, plant and machinery, vehicles, etc.
10. Value of redundant/replaced plant.
11. Project starting and expected completion dates.
12. Expected plant life.
13. Justification category; expansion, cost reduction, etc.
14. Evaluation horizon, years.
15. Cash flow due to project, per annum, average.
16. Method of computation: DCF, return on investment, payback.
17. Depreciation: method, rate, amounts.
18. Depreciation tax allowances.
19. After tax cash flow.
20. Project return (on the basis of 16).
21. Budget reference and provision (if any).
22. Remarks. These should include the key assumptions made and the implications if the project does not go forward.

### *Administrative and Control Requirements*

1. Manager submitting the document: role, signature, date.
2. Originator of document.
3. Specialists responsible for aspects of the project proposal.
4. Project evaluators.
5. Endorsement signatures, depending on route of presentation.
6. Authori sationlevel.
7. Decision: nature, date, signature.

### *Supporting Schedules*

1. Description of buildings, plant and processes.
2. Outline site, buildings or plant layout.
3. Main plant item list.
4. Specialist technical/operational evaluations and submissions: guarantees, planning consents, etc.
5. Procurement cash flow pattern and capital expenditure graph.
6. Project benefit: analysis and cash flow explanation.
7. Project design, engineering and management charges.
8. Project organisation.
9. Contingencies and provisions.

The list indicates the core operational inputs to the plant investment decision. There are further important specialist inputs in some industries. For instance, in the manufacture of chemical intermediates a forward contract to cover the plant output could be the most important document. What has been listed is the raw material for structured project presentation from operational levels. Specialist legal, financial, foreign exchange, taxation or other professional advice may also have to be sought for important projects. But usually the point of departure for this is a well-prepared operational proposition in the first place.

*Other Documents*

*Emergency request forms.* These are used if an emergency requires immediate action and the formal authorisation system needs to be short circuited. An emergency may arise from an accident or a major production breakdown. The document records the on-the-spot decision and verbal authorisation. It requires a statement of the emergency situation, the proposed course of action, its estimated costs and the authorised commitment level.

*Supplementary requests.* When the project costs are likely to exceed the authorised amount a supplementary authorisation/review system is usually actuated in respect of the additional expenditure. The form which gives expression to it requires an explanation of the changes involved or an account of the extra costs where the project remains unchanged. The administrative and control requirements of the original project submission are repeated and wherever possible authorisation should be at one level higher than the previous decision.

**The Character of the Authorisation Group**

It is relevant to the study of the authorisation process to look at the decision makers in their organisational setting. It is commonplace to designate such people as 'top management,' but this umbrella term hides a number of relationships. Perhaps the most useful way to show these is by actual examples.

In all cases the ultimate authority and responsibility for authorisation rested with the main board of directors of the company or group of companies concerned. Such authority can be divided into two categories:

1. Direct authority. This concerns the definition of the capital expenditure system and associated policies. It also refers to the actual decision making about projects as defined within the system (these are the projects above a stated minimum of size or import).
2. Delegated authority. This covers the decision making of groups or individuals subordinate to the main board, whose authority to make investment decisions could be instituted, varied or cancelled by the main board.

*Case Example A*

Since a merger in 1964 company A formed a division within a larger group. Ultimate authority rested with the board of the holding company. However, the relationships between company A and its parent reflected a large measure of decentralisation. Company A became a public company in 1935 and had acquired a position of prominence in its field. The development of its name, goodwill and general reputation was unaffected by the 1964 merger.

One of the reasons for this merger was the company's need to have stronger financial support for its expansion plans. The holding company provided and controlled this support. The group policy board, consisting of the group chairman, managing director, finance director and one non-executive director, made the major decisions. No directors from company A were on this committee.

Overall appropriations for capital expenditure were made on an annual basis but this did not prevent company A from making application for a specified project authorisation at any time. 75% of the company's annual depreciation cash flow could be applied within the discretion of the company; the remainder could be allotted by the group managing director as he thought appropriate.

It was interesting to note, as an example of the initiative afforded by decentralisation that the capital evaluation manual developed by company A was adopted by the whole of the group.

*Case Example B*

The history and the development of company B was different in character from company A. Its operation was more centralised and although the division, whose capital projects were investigated, was the major operating unit of the company in terms of turnover and profit, it had traded for many years under the company's name—in a sense, it generated the company image to the outside world. The executive director responsible for this, and an allied division, was on the main board of the company and its executive committee. This committee consisted of eight executive directors who met monthly with the managing director as chairman. The committee was responsible for running the day-to-day routine of the business of the company. Minutes of its meeting were discussed by the main board. Capital expenditure applications for projects up to £100000 were dealt with by the finance committee. Larger project applications had to be considered by the main board.

*Case Example C*

This company broadly doubled in size (assets, turnover, labour employed) during the period 1965-70. Much of this growth was due to a policy of acquisition. The company had developed a formal group structure and this account refers to its main subsidiary. The distinction between this subsidiary and the holding company was relatively fine, for the subsidiary was the original and the main operating unit of the group. Its chairman was the chairman of the holding company and its managing director was also on the main board. Three of the five main board members were on the board of the subsidiary. Despite its substantial size the company still had strong family associations and traditions and this was reflected in the board compositions. The two boards made the main investment decisions but their interlocking nature suggested that the same people were primarily involved.

*Case Example D*

The main decision group on capital investments was the board of the holding company, several members of which were formerly associated with the constituent businesses which merged in 1948 to form company D.

*Comment*

Some interesting points emerge from these case illustrations. Firstly, most of the decision makers seem to have been fulltime executives and as such were familiar with the operational context. Secondly, there was a tendency towards specialisation at board level as the detailed scrutiny of proposals was concerned. Thirdly, more than one board might be involved with authorisation, although effective power tended to be with one group of decision makers.

**The Delegated Authorisation of Capital Expenditure**

It was already noted that hundreds of projects might be authorised by a company of substance during its financial year. In most cases, the frequency and respective values of these projects conform broadly to a Pareto distribution, with the bulk of the projects being of small value and representing simple plant acquisitions. A standard practice relating to the delegated authorisation of minor capital expenditure is common in such circumstances. One can further observe a partial correlation between the level of authority within the hierarchy and the amounts which can be authorised. Limits are set on individual amounts as well as on cumulative or time rate expenditures. A typical pattern of delegation is shown on Table 3.1.

Such a tabulation can only be indicative. Overall company levels of capital expenditure vary considerably, not only

TABLE 3.1

**Some Patterns of Project Authorisation Limits**

| *Level* ↓ | *Pattern*→ *A* £ | *B* £ | *C* *Item in budget* £ | *Item not in budget* |
|---|---|---|---|---|
| Factory manager<br>Factory director | 2500 | 2000 | 2000 | 250 |
| Divisional director<br>Divisional managing director | 5000 | 5000 | 40000 | 10000 |
| Divisional committee<br>(below board level) | 25000 | — | — | — |
| Company managing director<br>(or deputy M.D.) | — | 10000 | — | — |
| Group managing director<br>or deputy | — | — | 100000 | 100000 |
| Board finance committee | — | 250000 | — | — |

because of the scale of operation, but also with the capital intensity of production processes. Furthermore, titles do not adequate indicate the standing of a particular organisational role within the overall structure. The object of a delegation system is to process the many small projects which in value constitute only a modest proportion of the total capital expenditure. Many routine projects reflect a given machine value category. Where technological factors are a significant determinant of project values this is often reflected by the authorisation framework. For instance, company B which operated standard production lines had many projects around the £10000 mark which usually involved a standard module for such a line. Divisional authorisation levels matched this project value. Different limits were often specified for various project categories. In one case there was no delegated authority for expansion projects; only for replacement and modernisation. Another important factor affecting discretion levels was whether or not the project was included in the capital expenditure budget.

Cumulative project authorisation limits were generally set by the annual capital expenditure budgets, broken down proportionately for each level of management. In a number of cases the permitted annual total seemed to be about five times the maximum individual project value.

On the whole, the extent of financial delegation below director level is relatively limited. While certain scope may be given to divisional boards, control at factory manager level tends to be tight. In larger companies the level of divisional discretion reflects performance in terms of return on capital employed. The time-lag effect of continuous inflation tends to erode the real worth of managerial autonomy despite the periodic increase of discretion limits.

## The Administrative Practice of Authorisation

Major projects are authorised at board meetings and the minutes of the meeting are the evidence of authorisation. In some cases there is a further signature by the chairman or managing director on the formal project document with or without reference to the board minute concerned. Where authorisation is delegated, the signature of the appropriate executive is usually sufficient.

In administrative terms authorisation sets off a number of tasks, such as formal notification of approval to the project applicants, the accounts and purchasing departments, the issue of job and accounts numbers, etc.

The authorisation process is not confined to mere yes/no decisions. For instance, a rejection could be combined with the request for one or several subsequent alternative submissions. Projects could be scaled down where a number of identical plant items were required. Where sequential cost commitments are involved the first stages could be approved and the remainder rejected or, more likely, deferred. Alternatively, the whole project could be postponed or deferred to a later board meeting, often with requests for additional information.

Authorisation does not always give automatic sanction to incur expenditure. Whilst with the more limited setting of the factory manager's financial discretion there is little point in delaying the authorised expenditure, the larger sums, greater complexity or uncertainty of the situation at main board level prompts some boards to apply finer controls of cash releases. Thus a 'tap' system of detail sanction within the global authorisation might be used by the board or an executive director for internal or external expenditure. Where the project engineering and design content is considerable the board may permit internal expenditure on such work, yet stop all external commitments. Often this is done to retain technologists who might in the short run be underemployed or redundant. It is a form of limited risk taking. The cost of such work is carried forward as part of the total project capital expense, or written off if in the end the project is abandoned.

In some instances there is also a time-lag in the operation of the tap system. The board formally accepts the commitment of the investment proposal but regards cash expenditure release as a separate decision problem.

In addition to the board's control of capital expenditure, administrative expenditure release systems could provide a further mechanism of authorisation and control. The practice of company C provides a good example. In support of project applications it was necessary to specify the required plant items and their costs in some detail Estimates were also submitted in respect of plant accessories, transport charges and installation costs. Similarly, building and engineering services costs were also to be tabled in an itemised form. Project authorisation included approval of the project scheme and plant item list. Subsequently, expenditure requisitions arising from the project had to be forwarded to the assistant group chief accountant for verification that the requisitions were in line with the proposed project scheme. Only then would commitments be authorised. The example also suggests that there is no precise boundary between authorisation as such and subsequent project financial control.

## Supplementary Authorisation

Where a project proposal has been sanctioned to the amount requested, the permission to spend further monies on the project is usually given by supplementary authorisations. Such additional sanction may be due to a variety of reasons. In most cases the extra expenditure is unattractive to the authorisation group. Quite apart from the administrative bother, it suggests that the proposal met with complications in implementation and the certain predictions were mistaken. More seriously, the economics of the project may be affected; the investment looks correspondingly less attractive.

The main causes of additional expense are as follows:

*General inflation effects* during the project duration. This is primarily seen in terms of higher labour costs and equipment charges. The increase in expense is a function of the project period.

*Equipment and design changes.* These are part of the process of full plant definition which may not be complete at the proposal stage. There could still be unresolved technical problems, the solutions of which turn out to be more expensive than first anticipated,

*Project implementation difficulties.* These are unexpected troubles which arise during the project execution. For instance, in factory construction an unprecedented storm causes a landslide and requires extensive remedial work.

*Project delays.* Where the project schedule is exeeeded and manpower resources need to be employed for longer than budgeted, then excess costs have to be absorbed.

*Improvements.* Two source categories can be established here. Where a project has an extended planning stage, particularly when linked with engineering/development work, there is the opportunity to incorporate improved versions of the plant or processes into the project. Extra costs are normally associated with these, not only because of the further call on resources but also due to the possible disturbance effects of their introduction into an ongoing project. The other source of improvement is within the project itself. It arises from the detailed definition work which is part of the project implementation. In that sense it is related to *Equipment and design changes* (above).

Extra expenses due to improvement are more acceptable and controllable than the other types. Nevertheless, there is the dilemma of choice between the benefits of effective project execution and the yield from the latest knowledge. If the improvement content is substantial it could lead to a major project reconstruction, or to a separate project.

### *Administrative Provision for Excess Expenditures*

The authorisation procedures for supplementary project expenditures can be divided into two distinct categories. The first is that of implicit authorisation. The authorisation group accepts the limits of estimate accuracy and the hazards of project implementation; it establishes an expenditure tolerance for minor overruns without re-actuating the whole submission and authorisation mechanism. The tightness of such tolerances is, of course, a matter of judgement and experience. For instance, company A specified ±5 per cent of the approved figure, company C permitted an excess of 10 per cent, company D an excess of £1000 or 5 per cent, whichever greater, of the capital value in respect of an existing project authorisation.

(These are non-inflation tolerances; separate provision would be required for inflation effects). Excess expenditure within the given limits did not reduce responsibility, but contained administrative work.

Where the amounts in question exceed the set limits, explicit authorisation is required and a supplementary capital expenditure request system is activated. Such a system is usually designed to focus attention on the reasons for excess expenditure In the excess expenditure situation one can isolate changes in project scope from other causes of over-expenditure. Such alterations in scope were reflected in the system of company C which required the notification to the assistant group chief accountant together with the relevant changes in costs. Changes in project scope were recognised as causes of excess expenditure by the other company systems, although not specifically referred to in their project documentation.

While changes in scope often increased project costs, or were used as a justification for this, there were instances where a reduction in expenditure resulted. In extreme cases a project might no longer be necessary. The systems operated by companies A and C allowed for such possiblities. With company A, requests for sanction to reduce or to cancel a project were required. In default of this the project originators would be held to the undertaking of their project submission.

A particular aspect of the supplementary request procedure is associated with project cost control. In most cases the request is made in anticipation of excess costs, bvt authorisation can also be retrospective to formalise excess expenditure already incurred.

**Check List: Project Presentation**

1. Have all forms been completed?
2. Is the supporting material available in submission form? Key specifications, plant lists, drawings?
3. Has all presentation liaison taken place with affected departments, particularly the accounting function?

4. Have all supporting signatures been obtained?
5. Have all code/accounting numbers been specified?
6. Have you checked the project submission category (if any)?
   (a) Already in Budget.
   (b) Extra to Budget.
   (c) 'Emergency.
   (d) Supplementary, etc.
7. At what authorisation level will the project be considercd?
8. Is there a submission timetable for this authorisation level?
9. What is the distribution list for project presentation?

4

# PROJECT ORGANISATION

## —An Analysis of Behavioural Skills

K. S. BHAT*

Organisation according to contemporary theory is a strategy for achieving a specified purpose. The traditional bureaucratic systems have been under constant pressure with new demands placed on them by a society in the process of growth and development. The rigid structure, hierarchy, power orientation, and operational procedures have often been found dysfunctional to new situations. "Some of the most perplexing and urgent problems of our time are not technological but human and organisational."[1] The harmful consequences of organisational inadequacies are all the more felt in a situation of 'maximum government'.

The inadequacies of traditional organisational systems to cope with innovative tasks is evident from the search for alternatives in organisational design. For "innovative tasks seem to require a new interplay of generations and a new

*Mr. K.S. Bhat is Deputy Director (Senior), LB Shastri National Academy of Administration, Mussoorie.

restructuring of hierarchical arrangements providing much greater freedom and mobility."[2] Again, one of the great institution builders of modern times, Dr. Homi Bhabha noted[3] that different tasks and institutions required different types of administrative practices, and that the transfer of government administrative practices either to industrial enterprises or research and development organisations, produced inefficiencies and lack of morale.

The concepts in organisational design have grown out of dissatisfaction with the ability of the existing organisations to cope with new tasks. The last decade has shown increased entrustment of development tasks and innovative programmes to project teams and task groups. The experience reportedly has been good and the continuation of this organi ational arrangement is indicative of the faith the policy formulating levels have on the new system. For optimal effectiveness, however, good structure alone is not enough. For "structures, procedures and techniques are important but these must be sustained by a cluster of attitudes, conveying care, trust and nurture on the part of responsible persons."[4] The present paper is an effort to examine the behavioural aspects for effective functioning in such project organisations. A theoretical framework of such an organisation is presented before the behavioural dimensions are explored.

*Theoretical Framework*

One way of classifying an organisation's character is on the basis of ideological orientation. The organisational ideology has a profound effect on organisational effectiveness. For, it basically determines how:

(a) decisions are made

(b) human resources are used, and

(c) the external environment (relevant environment) is approached.

Roger Harrison[8] lists four organisation ideologies*; *viz.*,

(i) Power orientation,

(ii) Role orientation,

(iii) Task orientation, and

(iv) Person orientation.

The ideologies are seldom found in their pure form in most organisations. But most organisations display distinct features of one or other of these organisational ideologies. On the basis of this typology, the traditional bureaucratic set up of public systems falls into 'power orientation' and 'role orientation' types. Bureaucracy by definition should normally have role orientation ideology, but in the practical functioning due to cultural, historical and personality factors, some of the sub-systems have preponderantly power orientation.

The power oriented organisation ensures tight control and integration. But when the organisation becomes large and complex, controls tend to break down. Under these conditions, the role oriented ideology is more effective since rules and procedures provide a high degree of internal integration.

**Power orientation*—Aggressive, attempting to dominate its environment and vanquish opposition. Within the organisation, those who are powerful strive to maintain absolute control over subordinates.

*Role orientation*—Emphasis is on legality, legitimacy, and responsibility. There is strong emphasis on hierarchy and status which is moderated only by the commitment to legitimacy and legality The system is slow to adopt change.

*Task orientation*—Task achievement is of highest value. Nothing is permitted to get in the way of task accomplishment. Authority is considered legitimate if it is based on appropriate knowledge and competence; it is not legitimate if it is based solely on power and position.

*Person orientation*—The organisation exists primarily to serve the needs of its members. The organisation is a device through which the members can meet the needs that they could not satisfy themselves, *e.g.*, consulting terms, small group of professionals, etc.

Under a person or task oriented ideology the internal cohesion is more difficult to achieve. Questions like—how are the efforts to be coordinated; what happens to the professionals after problem solving or task performance; what about long range planning and continuity of effort etc., crop up. If it is too stable, is there no danger of its becoming role oriented or power oriented?

The "matrix organisation" is a compromise answer to the problems of internal structure. In a matrix organisation the working groups are formed the normal pyramidal organisations. These individuals selected from different functions and different levels are assembled together as a relatively autonomous group. Structural stability is provided by a fixed role oriented framework organised on functional lines. Personnel are readily detachable from the functions for varying periods of time during which they join a task oriented work or project team. The career prospects, pay and promotions emanate from the role oriented aspect of the system.

The need for departure from the conventional line-staff concept has also been emphasised by Gerald Fisch who advocated functional team work concept.[6] That some of the effective organisations have moved towards this concept is an indication of the inadequacy of the conventional design of organisation.

The matrix organisation implies a departure from the pragmatic principle which has worked well—the oneman-oneboss principle. The member in a matrix organisation works under two bosses, acting under the direction of two different managements—one of the project team and the other from the functional group of which he is a member. In other words he becomes a member of two groups—one of the project and the other of the functional organisation from which he is drawn. The structure, therefore becomes non-linear.

The project management team or task force is a flexible alternative to the permanent staff structure, one in which the "organisation can be exactly engineered to fit each challenge." Warren G. Bennis predicted in 1969 that the organisations of future "will be adaptive, rapidly changing temporary systems, organised around problem to be solved by groups of relative strangers with diverse professional skills. . . they will evolve in response to problems rather than to programmed expectations. . . ."[7] The temperary organisational systems be they task groups or project teams are no longer organisations of the future. There is increasing evidence of these organisations in all spheres of work in private industry, public sector, scientific organisations and even in the government sector.

Having laid the theoretical framework of a matrix organisation, we can now examine how far the ongoing projects conform to this concept. The examination is confined only to limited areas though the analysis and the findings may go beyond this limited context. It is admitted that the project teams have variations depending on the nature of task, time frame and the type of personnel required, as for example, development tasks and scientific project teams seem to be requiring different composition and structural arrangements. In the case of scientific, engineering and R and D organisations, the tradition of temporary project teams is there since long, but the wider use of project concept in the traditional bureaucratic set up is of a more recent origin.

The concept of project management has grown out of the inability of functional organisations and its appendages to task on specific tasks, be they relating to, agricultural development, or programmes addressed to the amelioration of a specific target group like Small Farmers Development Agency, or Integrated Rural Development. The constitution of this organisational arrangement is also a recognition of inter-disciplinary nature of the task involved. Implicit in this is an admission of the problem of securing coordination between the various departments whose contributions in varying degrees are required for task accomplishment.

A typical organisational arrangement of a project constitutes a project officer, who is normally a generalist, and a number of professionals from agriculture, veterinary, irrigation, small scale industries, etc. departments. There are other variants of this structural arrangement. The professionals are engaged in the project on a part-time or full-time basis and during this period they work under the overall guidance of the project officer. In the arrangements envisaged the project officer has a key role to perform. As the chief executive officer he is "not only to ensure formulation of appropriate programmes with the technical officers but their effective implementation by securing assistance and cooperation of the concerned departments of the state government as also the fullest involvement of local administration and organisations."[8]

A detailed analysis of the responsibilities of a project officer would broadly reveal the following functions:

—Scanning the relevant environment;

—Deciding on the specific requirements;

—Formulating projects;

—Selling the 'projects' to the client groups;

—Implementation; and

—Obtaining feedback and correction.

In the nature of arrangements the project officer becomes a focal person with a focal role which has the key dimensions, namely,

(1) Managing the interface with (i) the client groups, (ii) the local organisations like Panchayat or other political bodies or administrative organisations, (iii) the higher administrative group consisting of district, state authorities.

(2) Effective coordination of the work of professionals from different departments.

The effectiveness of a project leader can be thought of as a function of his ability to manage the interfaces and to secure effective coordination of the various functional specialists of his team. The next section will deal with an analysis of the behavioural attributes for effectiveness in such a situation. Such as analysis is useful as by its very nature, function and composition, a project team cannot be effective if the values, work practices, the ideology, leadership style of a traditional bureaucratic organisation are imposed on it.

Management of the three interfaces listed earlier requires skills which go far beyond managing, say an office of an industrial enterprise. Firstly, there is the ability and sensitiveness to indentify the problems of the client groups. Secondly, the ability and skill to formulate appropriate detailed schemes or programmes, and lastly, the ability and skill to sell the idea to the client groups. It is obvious that these go much beyond the routine functioning of a bureaucratic.

A singnificant aspect here is the detaied knowledge of the economic and social coditions of the people, which in its extreme functional form is total identification by the project leader. For effectiveness either at the survey or the formulation level the knowledge base has to be beyond the 'text-book level'. The degree of sensitiveness shown by the project leader will be reflected in the schemes evolved and its implementation process through various stages.

One of the important skills is the ability to sell the projects, to transfer the idea from the file to the recipients. This aspect of work called extension work particularly while working in a tradition bound, poor and illiterate group requires besides skills, appropriate attitudes and knowledge.

The second and the more important dimension of effectiveness is the coordination that is to be achieved in the functioning of the project group. This assumes special singnificance in a matrix organisation because of its task nature and composition of the membership with its divided loyalty. Coordination in a matrix organisation cannot be silent acquiescence and compliance of orders from above. For, a project leader is dealing with professionals from other functional organisations and the situation is of one person-two bosses.

Predictably therefore if coordination is sought to be achieved by authoritarian commands, the reaction could be negative. The imposition of power orientation ideology or even role orientation therefore could become dysfunctional. As long as "administration is thought as a power system rather than a technical collaborative system, coordination will cause trouble."[9]

Crucial to the success of any project or task team therefore is the coordination achieved by the project leader in directing the energy of the members to the task performance. The proper use of control systems can direct the energy to motivate the employees to higher level of performance, better quality of output. The wrong use of control systems can produce dysfunctional consequences, such as game playing, manipulating the results, beating the system, or generally increasing the entropy of the system. The distinguished scientist and organisation builder, Dr. Vikram Sarabhai wrote: "In professional groups comprising scientists, engineers, and others it is important to recognise that motivation and control is largely inherent and contained in professional commitments, In organisations using large professional groups, the role of aminiistration has largely become one of service and not of-control. This requires a basic change in attitudes rather than a change in procedures and practices."[10]

This would imply that the project leader has to depend largely on internalised control systems,[11] such as job satisfaction job challenges, acceptance of project goals rather than imposed or legal controls.

A crucial role is played by the project leader in motivating the other members and in creating a feelling of "wantedness". The process of alienation can be triggered off easily in a matrix organisation leading to dysfunctional, non-synergistic behaviour This can be countered only by stregthening the linkages of the individual to the project and the project group.

It is worthwhile at this stage to examine the concepts linking individuals with the project and bringing in to focus the factors that have influences on their behaviour.

The figure (next page) gives a two dimensional view of the influence on individual in a project team. By joining a project the individual enters into a psychological contract with (i) the team (ii) the team leader, (iii) the project itself. The concepts

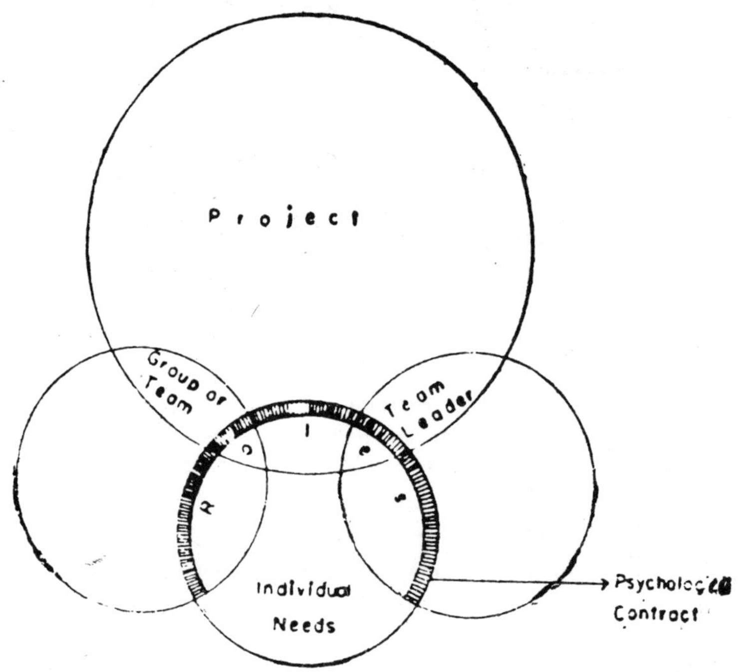


Diagram adapted from Geoffrey Hutton, "Individuals in Enterprises" in *Organisation Restructuring* London, McGraw-Hill, p 184.

linking him to the project which influence his behaviour can be described as:

(i) psychological contracts

(ii) the role set consisting of the role expectations of

(a) the project leader

(b) the project group, and

(c) his parent organisation.

The other major influence on his behaviour is his own needs and the extent to which the project helps him to fulfil them.

Working in a project, problems can arise on account of strains in the psychological contract with the project, the project leader or the project team itself. It is also possible that role conflict may develop. This can happen if the stated role are conflicting and contradictory. One can, for example, visualise a conflict situation arising out of conflicting role expectations placed on the individual by his parent functional organisation and by the project leader or the group. This is a distinct possibility in situations where functional department tend to work as closed systems.

The effectiveness of groups should also be found in the interaction process that takes place among members as they work on the task. At one extreme, for example, the group members may work together so badly that members do not share the information that is critical to the solution of the problem in hand, and the outcome suffers. On the other hand, the group members may work in harmony, leading to synergistic solutions to problems and creative work. In creating the conditions of harmony the project leader has a focal role to play.

The above analysis clearly rules out power oriented or role oriented ideology for project groups or task teams. The ideology necessarily has to be task orientation and this suggests itself the following four task effectiveness elements:

(i) Combating alienation—Strengthening the psychological contracts with the project;

(ii) Motivation through use of internalised control systems;

(iii) Breaking down of hierarchical barriers; and

(iv) Positive interaction between the members of the group.

In any group a distinction can be made between two sets of activities—one set of activities of the members of the group which have to do with the achievement of the goals of the group and the other set of activities which have to do with group maintenance. Goal achievement activities include goal emphasis, *i.e.*, setting goals and repeated emphasis on their achievement, and work facilitation, such as supplying technical knowledge, planning, scheduling, and providing the required resources. Group maintenance consists of support activities, *i.e.*, encouraging people and making it easier for them to cooperate with each other and adopt a win-win approach. These behavioural patterns become all the more significant for success in a matrix organisation like a project group, which is semi-autonomous in character. For such a group to be effective, it is essential that both task related activities and the maintenance related functions are performed well by the focal person.

Underlying this paper is the assumption that there is concern for optimisation of project resources and that democratic values are pervasive. The broad conclusions regarding behavioural skills that emerge out of this analysis suggest a task ideology for project groups. More importantly, it brings out the dysfunctional aspect of role or power oriented ideology. Adoption of task orientation ideology calls for styles of functioning, which are alien to bureaucratic ethos. As Roger Harrison puts it, "Role oriented people cannot be plugged into a task oriented system without conflict."[12] Apparently for projects to work well, people have to be chosen and trained with care.

## REFERENCES

1. Chowdhry. Kamla, *Change-in-Organisations*, Bombay, Lalvani, 1970.

2. . . . . . "Institution-Building and Social Change", *Indian Journal of Public Administration*, Vol. XIV. No. 4, 1968, pp. 943-961.

3. . . . . . ., (Ed.) *Management for Development*, New Delhi, Vikas.

4. . . . . . . . . . . . *Change-in-Organisations*, op. cit.

5. Harrison, Roger, "Understanding Your Organisation's Character'" *Harvard Business Review*, May-June, 1972.

6. Gerald-Fisch, "Line and Staff is Obsolete", *Haivard Business Review*, September-October, 1961.

7. Bennis, Warren G., "Post-Bureaucratic Leadership," *Transaction*, July-August 1969.

8. Quoted from the Report on Evaluation Study of Small Farmers, Marginal Farmers and Agricultural Labourers Projects—1974, 75, Programme Evaluation Organisation, Govt. of India, p. 10.

9. Guy Hunter "*The Administration of Agricultural Development—Lessons from India*,', Oxford Uniervsity Press, p. 29.

10. Chowdhry, Kamla, *Management for Development*, *New Delhi*, Vikas, pp. 26-27.

11. Katz and Kahn, *The Social Psychology of Organisations*, New York, John Willey & Sons, 1966.

12. Harrison, Roger, op. cit.

# 5

# PROJECT IMPLEMENTATION

'The project is on!' This watershed phrase, followed by the countersigned project application form or a special letter of authorisation, marks the beginning of the next stage of the investment process—the project implementation stage. For the sake of simplicity we shall assume an uncomplicated authorisation process—on conditional or part authorisation—an unqualified agreement to a direct request.

Project implementation is concerned with the realisation of the first part of the project intention, *i.e.*, the provision of the physical facilities needed to generate the desired economic performance. This first-stage objective itself has to be achieved within set technical, operational, financial and timetable terms. This task of such achievement is often given to those who develop the project justification in the first instance—with many companies this is a matter of policy. It is thus common to see members of the project preparation group subsequently concerned with implementation. There are, of course, significant benefits of continuity with such an arrangement. The actual mix will vary with project and company; there is a division of labour, very much affected by project size between specialist estimators and full-time project engineers.

Just as there is likely to be a carry-over of people from the preparation to the implementation stage, so there is an element of continuity in the organisational framework. This chapter is first concerned with the systems aspects of project implementation. It then considers some aspects of project control with particular reference to two major project criteria: time and cost.

## The Concept of Project Implementation

This part of the overall investment process is mainly described in textbooks on project management. Such books are couched in normative terms; they are designed to help the practitioner. It is not our intention to emulate them in detail, yet our account would be incomplete if no reference were made to the organisational and physical activities which constitute the very process of investment. The progress of authorised projects, especially those of major significance to the well-being of the firm, remains the ultimate concern of the project authorisation group. Here come the first feedback signals on the venture. The fortunes or otherwise of the implementation stage colour the judgement of the decision makers and thus influence their attitudes towards new investment proposals. Theories of investment take no account of projects already authorised by the firm but still in the implementation stage. Yet some projects may take years to implement and their prolongation, beyond the set schedule and for whatever reason, can have major cash flow implications.

A brief description of the implementation stage is therefore desirable and it is perhaps most of convenient if this is expressed in systems terms Figure 5.1 illustrates the various constituents of this part of the total investment process. The implementation stage begins with the project brief and ends with the plant handover to the operating group which will commission the completed plant. The boundary between these two stages is not always clearly defined, but usually project implementation represents a capital cost, whereas commissioning costs are generally treated as an operating expense.

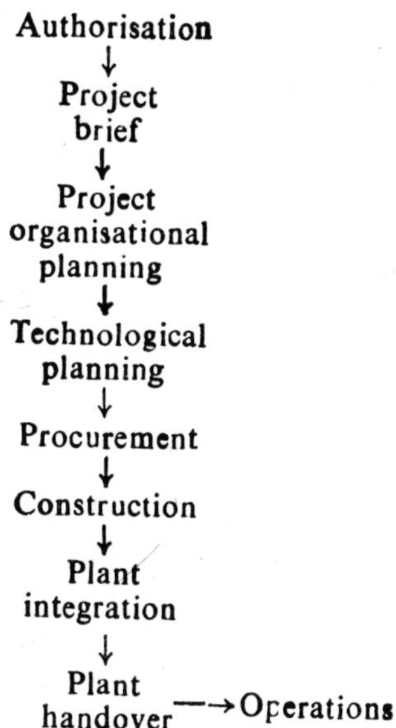


**Figure 5.1** Simplified block diagram for project implementation

*The Project Brief*

The project brief is the actuating mechanism of the implementation stage. Its format may be a standard document or a specific memorandum. It normally comes from the authorisation group and is addressed to the managers responsible for project implementation. The project brief can be regarded as having three distinct functions. Firstly, it is an instruction, a command, that something shall be done. Secondly, it provides such information as may be needed to clarify what has to be done. In practice, this usually means reference to the project proposal itself, which on authorisation becomes the framework for action. Additional information may be given, such as target dates or cash release programmes. Thirdly, the project brief can serve as evidence of authorisation to use company resources up to specified amounts. Depending on the nature of the project, the brief itself often reflects a dialogue between members of the authorisation group and the designated project manager.

*Project Organisational Planning*

The project which receives relatively prompt authorisation has the advantage of continuity; the project preparation group may not yet be disbanded and its members diverted to other tasks. This does not mean that they will be automatically chosen for the next stage; but very often they are, If the majority of the group are thus transferred the organisational framework is often also carried forward, at least in principle. The major difference between the preparation and implementation stages is the scale of project operation. This has organisational implications. Apart, perhaps, for the development biased project with a large technical content, most of the detailed work of implementation is understandably avoided at the preparation stage. Once a measure has been obtained of the technical risks, resources commitment at the preparation stage is conditioned by the likehood of authorisation. There is little point in major expenditures before a decision has been made. But now, after authorisation, a project group might have to grow tenfold. The framework of operation, if not available from previous comparative projects, must be quickly established. This is the purpose of the project organisational planning stage.

The main constituents of this project planning stage are given below. Although listed here in sequence some will be developed concurrently in practice. The context of a major project will be presumed, say, one worth other £1000000 at 1970 prices. The same framework may hold for smaller projects, but would then be rather less formalised.

*Project organisation.* This is concerned with the definition of the project management role and the appointment of the project manager and his assistants. It settles the project structure, *i.e.*, the manner in which the project is to be carried out. For instance, it decides whether the project manager is to be a line manager with specialist staff directly responsible to him or whether his task is to coordinate and progress the work of specialists answerable to their own functional managers.

*Project systems definition.* This is the specification of all administrative procedures relating to the project. It establishes the pattern of information flow and the manner of coordination within which specialist contributions are integrated to achieve the overall project objectives. The manner of project reporting and control in terms of time and money is particularly important here.

*Project representation.* We are concerned here with the formal relationships between the project group, through its management, and other interested parties. These relationships can be seen as an extension of the project systems. For instance, with top management they would be concerned with the manner of cost and progress reporting, cash flow requirements, etc. The relationship with the client department, factory or division may be expressed in detailed formal procedures. The client group is the internal organisational unit which will operate the plant furnished by the project. If it is a profit centre it will pay, internally, for the project costs. However, most of the dialogue will concentrate on technical, operational and schedule matters. The third major relationship is with contractors and plant suppliers. This can vary in range from the detailed definition of procedures with one main contractor, as is the practice in some process industries, to some general principles applicable to a wide spectrum of different contracts.

*Project framework planning.* It is an aspect of initiative, which is part of project management, to take the overall project objectives, as defined in the implementation brief, and to break these into meaningful sub-targets for both internal and external project contributors. In essence, these are scheduling tasks if they involve time, or budget apportionments if they relate to costs. In practice, these may be linked. Thus a section of electrical engineers, working on a chemical plant project, might be given a budget for electric motors and starters, equivalent to 8 per cent of the overall project estimate, an engineering time budget of 1000 hours and a time scale of equipment delivery and installation which is integrated within an overall project programme. It is this type of detailed decision making, related to the planning of project execution, which is the most prevalent activity of the first phase of the project implementation stage. Much of the project success will depend on the thoroughness of this work.

Textbooks on project management have given mucb attention to the techniques available for this planning task. Particularly important here are network analysis techniques such as CPM (critical path method), PERT (programme evaluation review technique), PERT/COST; all of which are suitable for computer use. Line balancing and resource scheduling are other important oids for this planning stage. It is not possible to develop these techniques here and the interested reader is advised to consult the works of such writers at Moder and Phillips,[1] Hajek[2] and Hackney.[3] Suffice it to say that these techniques havehad a significant effect on the management of large projects and that it is one of the skills of a project manager to specify not only what techniques are to be used but also the manner and extent of their application. The techniques have their costs, of course, but the benefits from more effective project management and control more than justify these.

One general point needs to be made about some of the listed organisational planning activities. Where the scale and frequency of operation justifies it these will be pre-planned and defined as general practice for all projects over a given size, *i.e.* there is an organisational tooling-up which reduces the content of such activities in the typical project.

*Technological Planning*

This stage is primarily concerned with engineering and design. The project technical objectives, to whatever extent established so far, have now to be defined in detail and fully developed.

There can be great variation in the amount of technological planning required by a project. It can vary from almost nothing, in the case of a repeat project, to the largest project expense, when there is a high development content. Its main constituents can be listed briefly as follows:

*Process definition.* In systems terms the inputs and outputs for the plant are often specified in the project intent. The method of conversion from one to the other needs now to be spelled out. Typically, this is carried out in terms of a standard notation, such as flow diagrams (chemical industry), circuit diagrams (electronics) or process charts (engineering manufacture). The whole of the project content will be described in this way to obtain an overall view and to assess the interaction effects of constituent sections.

*Process and engineering design.* This comprises the functional and engineering design of all those project constituents for which a proprietary design is not available for technical or commercial reasons. The design need not be carried out by the firm; it can be contracted out to consultants or suppliers. But the task of verification or design approval still remains in such cases. Design in this context includes detail draughting as well as the construction of models. It can cover a wide range of technological skills. The design activity itself can be viewed as a hierarchy of complexity ranging from the total technological assembly of major units down to the last small component.

*Specification development.* Within our context of production plant a technical sp:cification is a statement about the expected character of an item of equipment, including its mode of construction where this is relevant. In terms of performance it will be concerned with such aspects as size, output rates, operational speeds, accuracy, reliability, etc. A particular environment may be specified in which such a performance is to be expected. The design requirements may dwell on basic matters of construction and such features which are important for operation, safety and maintenance. Separate specifications may be needed for installation and site construction work, acceptance testing, etc. Technical specifications usually form part of the contract conditions for procurement purposes.

*Equipment selection.* This activity is a natural follow-on from the specification task. It can also be a concurrent activity when the technical specification is required to structure the selection process. Equipment selection is seen here primarily as a technical rather than as a commercial choice; the latter is part of the procurement task. The specification sets the profile of technical requirements; equipment selection is the shortlisting of proprietary plant which can match the chosen profile. In such a profile construction one can distinguish between primary and secondary attributes. Primary attributes are those which reflect the very purpose of the plant and as such are not regarded as 'negotiable.' The secondary attributes are concerned with desirable but not essential features, and their selection is more affected by price considerations.

In essence then, equipment selection sets the boundaries within which the procurement decision has to be made. It is of course possible with specialist applications that the boundaries leave room for only one proposition. If no proposition is left, then there is no suitable proprietary equipment and the firm may be forced to develop its own plant. With effective project preparation such a possibility should have been anticipated.

### *Procurement*

Procurement consists of the acquisition of all plant, materials and external services required for a project. It involves the purchase of proprietary equipment, the negotiation of construction projects, indeed, anything which commits the firm in contrast, be it from a small fitting to a multi-million-pound agreement. It is not confined to the buying act but includes all contractual relationships until the close of a transaction. Procurement can be responsible for over 90 per cent of the project cash outflow. It is a key activity in the implementation stage which needs to be effectively integrated within the overall project system. Where the scale of operation warrants it, this form of procurement is organisationally separated from the purchase of materials for ongoing production operations. Within the project time scale, procurement follows the technological planning activity which, in the first instance, defines the type of equipment to be bought.

*Construction*

It is common project experience that as the planning work declines the centre of attention and activity shifts to the physical project execution—construction. This is no coincidence, but the logic of the project structure; construction only becomes a meaningful activity when its course has been charted, when all the relevant planning has been completed. Construction covers all building and related activities from trial test boring on a new, 'greenfield' factory site to the final landscaping. It tncludes the construction of production plant *in situ*, such as a new furnace, and the installation of equipment in specified positions. It can also involve temporary works such as road diversions, site workshops and construction personnel facilities. The site may be distant from the planning office; the workforce may be that of the firm or, more likely, employed by independent contractors.

The physical input of the construction activity tends to overshadow the other project implementation stages. Yet its success is largely a function of its predecessors. This does not deny the other important ingredient that has now to be furnished by the project group—effective site management. Where major construction schemes may employ hundreds, even thousands, where labour forces have to be built up, changed in mix and run down at rates which are unthinkable in most fields of production—in such cases there is a premium on the skills of work planning, coordination and control, skills which are the hallmark of good site management.

### *Plant Integration*

This is to some extent a continuation of the construction stage, and its segregation may seem somewhat artificial. Yet this work has a different emphasis. Consider walking past a public building under construction. The physical erection of the shell seems to be a comparatively quick process. This is then followed by an apparently long period when the building is there but still incomplete. This is the time when the empty shell is transformed for meaningful occupation; when the electricians, telephone people and plumbers are active. Similarly with production plant. The 'hardware' is there but it is now to be integrated into an overall production unit. The transcription can involve the feed and offtake of materials from machines, conveyors, chutes, pipes, power and control circuits, instrumentation, warning devices, etc. It is such items which change a collection of machines or process points into a complete production system. The ultimate in this is the fully-automated production unit. In a very rough sense we can say then that the construction stage is concerned with the 'brawn' of production, whereas this stage is associated with the 'brains' of the process.

### *Plant Handover*

We come now to the last phase of the project implementation stage, as defined. The capital expenditure has been incurred; a new production unit is physically ready to go into service. The handover, *i.e.*, the change of responsibility, is from the project group to operating management. In most cases where there is this division of labour, members of the operating staff nevertheless take the opportunity to acquaint themselves with the new plant during the latter stages of construction and plant integration. The nearer the plant gets to the operational state the more relevant become operational aspects and the participation of the operating groups.

In formal terms the handover takes place at an instant of time, but in practice the process can be extended. With large projects the handover can be by instalments, operating personnel move in as construction labour works itself out. The handover process can include the witnessing of tests, the calibration and setting of instruments and control devices, the physical check-out of equipment. Apart from buildings, plant, spares and accessories, the handover also covers documents which may be furnished with the equipment such as key drawings and maintenance manuals.

## Project Control

We have already mentioned that project implementation is an objective to the achieved within the constraints of technical and operational specifications, a project budget and timetable. The aim of project control is to ensure that these set boundaries are not overstepped. If, because of some unforeseen event, these limits have to be breached then it will be the function of the control system to warm and to inform so that steps may be taken to minimise such deviations.

The principle of control is a basic principle of management, and project control is similar to the control of any other business activity. It will differ in detail from other operational control systems for two reasons. Firstly, unless the scale of operation and the level of investment is very large, the capital project activity may be intermittent. Secondly, as we have already noted at the project preparation stage, functional responsibilities for capital projects are less clearly defined than, say, for manufacturing activities. A well-designed control system generally encompasses the following project aspects:

1. Expenditures and commitments to date, giving both totals and breakdowns to specified project accounting codes. These are compared, as far as possible, with the budget forecasts for the level of progress reached.
2. Expenditure forecasts to project completion, giving details and reasons for any overruns.
3. Progress in relation to programme.

4. Completion date forecast.
5. Project developments which might affect the technical and operational prospects of the completed plant.
6. Manpower/manhour analysis of all staff employed on the project.

The design of project reporting procedures reflects the emphasis a firm may give to these various control parameters. This also governs the manner and frequency of reporting. The first level is that of the project manager who is responsible for the detailed disposition of the project resources. The second is the top management level which monitors the overall project performance.

With the four companies the financial project control system was the most explicit. Companies C and D incorporated their control requirements in their capital expenditure manuals. Typically, project financial reports were required on a four-weekly or monthly basis. Aggregate reports on overall capital budgets and expenditures were similarly asked for from the various factories or cost centres. Other facets of reporting such as on programme progress seemed less developed. Many of the small to medium capital projects consisted of plant purchases where the company was hostage to delivery promises from suppliers. With extended deliveries the monthly progress report had little to tell. Major projects of a composite nature or with a substantial design/development content often had a specific progress reporting system linked with the monthly financial statements.

A particular facet of the overall control system was the administrative procedure relating to individual project commitments. For instance, with approved projects, company C insisted that all factory purchase requisitions were checked by head office accountants against the project proposal plant list before orders could be placed. Direct labour commitments were similarly verified by factory accountants. Company D required its factory chief accountants to make sure that prescribed practices relating to engineering contracts were followed by the appropriate staff. These concerned the placing of orders, acceptance of invoices, the precise responsibilities for installation, erection and the commissioning of plant. For contracts over £10000 instructions referred to the terms of payment, price variation formulae as well as the terms for sub-contractors. Particular attention had also to be given to the procedure and authority for ordering and accepting contract modifications and additions, the provision of site facilities and rules covering hygiene, catering, union conditions, etc. These examples suggest that administrative procedures can operate as important project control devices. They also limit the discretion available to the project manager.

**Indicators of Implementation Performance**

A review of the effectiveness of project implementation depends on supporting data. Such information is however hard to get. For a proper empirical study a set of implementation attributes would need to be established and a number of projects related to these. The great problem is to obtain the type of systematic information which provides the basis for inter-company generalisations. Samples cannot be chosen at random, the availability of data is the qualification for inclusion. The project sizes vary greatly; the politics of decision making cannot always be assumed away; behavioural aspects provide a set of variables which are difficult to isolate. We have all the complications of a multifactor, dynamic situation. Nevertheless, despite all this some meaning can be attached to two specific indicators: time and money.

*Capital Costs*

What follows is based on a more detailed scrutiny of the project accounts for twenty-eight new plant projects in four different companies. Projects ranged in value from just under £20000 to over £3 million (1970 prices). The ratio of actual project cost/

initial project authorisation was taken as the basic financial indicator. Values greater than 1 therefore indicate an overrun. The investigation was carried out at a time when the average annual rate of inflation in terms of the index of wholesale prices for mechanical engineering products was somewhat over 2 per cent.

The minimum observed ratio value was 0.672 and it was found here and in other cases where ratio values were appreciably below 1 that projects had been curtailed. It seems that with an extended project schedule and discrete plant units a company could change the project scope without undue disturbance losses. In such cases project authorisations are revoked, cancelling financial provisions which had not yet become commitments.

The maximum ratio value of 2.150 concerned a project with a heavy development content. Other cases of overrun also indicated development complications. Interestingly, these are not always within the company. They may be the immediate responsibility of an equipment supplier but still involve the company in consequential costs. Overall, the observations suggest that as the technical development content increases, project cost prediction also becomes more difficult. The closer a project comes to a research and development proposition the more opposite are Mansfield's findings[4] about the divergence between estimated and actual project costs. The technical risks are greater and this shows in project cost overruns. One might argue that with fuller project preparation such costs might be reduced. Admittedly, the project accounts can gain but this does not necessarily yield much of an overall saving to the company.

Irrespective of cause, project delays increased the chances. of excess project costs, quite apart from inflation effects The spread of project ratio values within a company also sheds light on its investment activities. For instance, the nine projects from one company had value ratios from 0.950 to 1.060. The company had a tight system of project financial control.

Apart from one major factory scheme, however, most of its projects were of modest value, comparatively short duration and constituted mainly proprietary equipment. With a given level of organisational effectiveness, the nearer projects come to the 'shopping basket' type, the closer should the outturn be to the original estimate.

As an indicator of implementation effectiveness, project costs are a useful guide provided allowance is made for:

1. late invoices and contingent liabilities;
2. changes in project content;
3. interrelated projects where cost transfers are sometimes made for 'in-house' reasons.

*The Project Time Scale*

Earlier in this chapter we included in the project implementation stage all those constituents from the project brief to the plant handover. The time lapse from the beginning of the former to the end of the latter would then constitute the project time scale. It is this parameter of project performance which we wish to consider further, both in terms of intention and of achievement.

*Problems of definition.* The terms: project time scale, project period, do not present serious conceptual problem, particularly if they can be related to specified systems of the type outlined in Figure 5.1. However, a number of interpretation and measurement problems affect their use in analysis. The point may be made by some examples from the twentyeight projects studied in detail.

One project had no time schedule. It was authorised only near the end of the physical plant construction process. Commitments were undertaken on the basis of personal understandings between senior executives of the main contracting companies and their client. Work proceeded on that basis;

authorisation and formal confirming orders came only towards the close of the work tasks. The detailed project correspondence left no doubt about the commitment and the implied contract, inferable from the conduct of the parties, would have been sustained in law. Whilst, perhaps, this was the most outstanding example of 'pre-authorisation commitment,' similar tendencies were also noted with some other projects. Such informal commitment, before the actual board decision, reveals interesting aspects of organisational behaviour.

A futher complication arose with some plant development and construction projects. In technical terms it was difficult to draw the line between development work before authorisation and the full equipment design subsequent to it. Project time scale definition became even more difficult when subsequently some of the pre-authorisation development costs were capitalised as part of the project costs. The project starting point could thus be redefined retrospectively.

At the other end of the project period technical and operating problems at the commissioning stage were the source of funther difficulties. The periods of project execution and plant commissioning could overlap, particularly with those large projects where handover to production could be on a stage-by-basis Failure or troubles at commissioning might force the project team and contractors to spend further time on plant modification, in some instances after they had already left the construction/installation site. Where there were no formal 'handover' documents, it was necessary to infer from the withdrawal of construction/installation labour that the project was physically complete for operational purposes.

It should not be inferred, of course, that every project time scale has such problems. However, it is important to be on one's guard when generalising from such data.

*The scheduled project period.* In the evaluation of the scheduled project period it is important to remember the background of a project. Where the project is confined to plant aspects and is unhampered by other time considerations, then the project schedule becomes a timetable for technological planning, procurement and installation work. The project schedule may however by affected by non project factors.

For instance, one project concerned major plant modifications the costs of which were capitalised. An important operational requirement was to maintain at all times adequate production capacity to meet the company's sales commitments. There had to be sufficient excess plant to production requirements to release machines for modification. Because of the nature of the product and its distribution costs such excess plant could not necessarily be aggregated on a group basis, *i.e.*, a particular factory had to be able to release a given machine. It was this which governed the project time scale, not the actual work content.

Another extraneous influence on the project time schedule is capital rationing. In one project all the plant could have been procured and installed within a few months. However, project cash release was determined by overall cash flow considerations and this more than doubled the project period.

Apart from this type of extra-project factor one can broadly relate the scheduled project period to the following:

1. the project size,
2. its technical and development content,
3. the delivery periods of key equipment.

For the reasons already stated, such relationships can only be regarded as approximate.

*Time schedule performance.* As with project costs a similar ratio can be used for the time dimension. It will now be the ratio of the actual to the scheduled project period. The scheduled project periods ranged from three tothirty-six months. The longest actual period noted came to sixty months but as work on it and finance for it were intermittent, the project was somewhat of a special case. About 60 per cent of all the projects were completed to schedule. The best time ratio of 0.667 reflected project curtailment. When overruns took place they were substantial in actual and in ratio terms. Time ratios of 2.5 and 2.4 were noted for specialist but proven proprietary equipment and this exceeded the overruns of incompany development-type plant projects. Three of the four projects with major development content exceeded their schedules.

With small samples only tentative conclusions are possible. As with costs, it seems, however, that an increase in project development content makes schedule prediction more difficult. Also, delays with suppliers and contractors, irrespective of technical task content, can at times be seriously underestimated.

**Check List: Project Implementation**

1. Who is responsible for the implementation of the project ?
2. To whom does he report?
3. What personal qualities, skills and experience would you seek in a project manager, project engineer? How do you dissect his track record?
4. Does the project brief specify the total approved expenditure, the project engineering and management fee?
5. What is the specified project completion date?
6. Is the project brief otherwise clear as to what will be expected? Where a project submission includes alternatives—has the choice been made and stated?
7. Is the project manager's role clearly defined?
8. Are there standard project procedures for guidance on project planning, scheduling, coordination, costing and control practice?
9. Have the relationships between the project group and 'project client' been examined, defined?

10. Have you carried out a project systems audit ? If not, take a machine specification or a layout drawing. Who should get a copy, who should be consulted, who should approve it ? Describe all aspects in a block diagram form. Are there gaps of inconsistencies?

11. What management techniques are used for project planning and control?

12. Do you ever audit the use of these techniques and look for a better cost/benefit ratio?

13. To what extent are major suppliers/contractors integrated with your project system? What is the communications framework?

14. How are the physical tasks of construction organised, managed and controlled?

15. Have relationships been adequately defined between site staff and the project section?

# 6

# THE PLANT INVESTMENT PROCESS

This chapter takes a first view at investment in production plant at the level of the company. To start with, the meaning of production plant will be more fully developed. The diverse activities and decision stages which form the plant investment process are then integrated within a systems approach. The planning and implementation of plant investment propositions goes on within the framework of company policies; the link, therefore, between the directing level and execution on 'capital account' is of special interest. Similarly, attention needs to be given to the interaction between those engaged on capital projects and those involved at various levels with day-to-day operations.

Where appropriate, discussions of principle will be amplified in this and following chapters by illustrations drawn from relevant industrial and research experience. The writer had the good fortune of access to plant investment work at a number of manufacturing companies. Reference will be made to work with four major companies. Two of these, companies A and B, are in the engineering industry, company C is in the glass industry, while company D is engaged in food production. The published accounts of these companies suggest that they belong to the more successful sector of their industries if such standing is measured in terms of size, profit and retrun on capital. All had large capital expenditure programmes. Although there were significant differences in procedures between the companies, each had given considerable thought to the management of its investment process and had evolved a standard practice.

**The Meaning of Industrial Investment**

Anyone who has observed the pattern of expenditure of an industrial firm will note the variety of goods and services which it obtains in the normal course of business. Disregarding such day-to-day operational payments as for materials, of salaries and other routine disbursements related to the process of manufacture, one can discern a variety of expenditures associated with a longer-term intent. These constitute investments in some form. The following is a brief summary of the more important categories of such expenditure:

(i) the purchase of production plant and the manufacture of tools;

(ii) the acquisition of land and the purchase or erection of buildings such as factories, warehouses, offices;

(iii) the purchase of all types of vehicles;

(iv) the acquisition of 'administrative aids', such as computers;

(v) planned increases in stock levels;

(vi) research and development projects;

(vii) the acquisition of patents and manufacturing licences;

(viii) investments in or the acquisition of other firms;

(ix) general portfolio investment.

All these categories have a common characteristic: they consist of expenditures from which future benefits or revenues are expected. The motivation for the expenditure is the criterion; future benefits may not always be realised. Except perhaps, for (v) and (vi) the firm usually requires capital funds for such expenditures, hence the term: capital expenditure.

In the United Kingdom, in accordance with Schedule 2 of the Companies Act 1967, companies are required to identify separately in their balance sheets fixed assets, current assets and those assets which are neither fixed nor current. In accounting terms it is the acquisition of these assets which can be regarded as investment, The term *capital expenditure*, as a sub-category investment, will henceforth be confined to the acquisition, improvement or modification of fixed assets.

**Investment for Production**

As to the investment expenditures already listed, this book confines itself to the capital expenditures which have some relevance to production. Production is taken here to include all those manufacturing tasks, including packaging, which make an article ready for sale within the normal practice of an industry. The transport or storage of finished products, as part of the distribution function, is excluded form this. The expenditures may be directly related to production, such as the purchase of machines, or indirectly in the from of building projects to house such equipment. Some categories are partially relevant; for instance, vehicles could comprise lorries for inter-factory transport and thus be directly concerned with production or they could be vans for retail distribution.

Administrative investments, say in computers and computer systems, tend to cut across functional boundaries. Admittedly, a computer specifically installed for the purpose of process control or production control is immediately relevant, but the majority of computers in industry tend to be applied first to accounting and commercial routines and to furnish general management information. Established originally in these activities, there is a tendency to broaden their role to the functional area of production. In many instances such widening of application was part of the original but not necessarily quantified purchase justification. The advent of the micro-processor is likely to bring computers much closer to production. Their relatively modest cost permits the development of decentralised computer systems containing a number of such units. This will be helped by the growing number of production staff trained in their operation.

Research and development expenditure, if capitalised, is relevant as for as it applies to production processes and leads to new or revised types of plant. This refers particularly to detailed machine design which can be expensive in draughting hours. Fundamental product investigations, although likely to have manufacturing repercussions, are not included. Again, investments in, or the acquisition of, other firms are only relevant if the objectives are related to production, such as the need to extend manufacturing capacity.

It is interesting to relate this approach to the national statistics relating to fixed capital expenditure of manufacturing industry. Table 6.1 indicates that about 76 per cent fixed of capital expenditure is devoted to plant and machinery. The expenditure on new building work, at 18 per cent, is relatively modest. Such expenditures are mainly a function of new factory building or major capacity expansion programmes. Often increased output, due to more up-to-date equipment, needs no more operating space than the previous process. The constant 1970 prices reveal the decline in the volume of investment which has taken place since that year.

## The Plant Investment Process

This consists of all the activities concerned with plant investment. The process starts with tentative ideas and finishes with their ultimate realisation in terms of effective, operating production plant. The various process constituents are shown in a simplified form in Figure 6.1. They form part of the three main process stages: preparation, decision and implementation.

TABLE 6.1

**Fixed Capital Expenditure of UK Manufacturing Industry at 1970 Prices (£ million)**

| *Year* | *Total* | *Plant and machinery* | *New building work* | *Vehicles* |
|---|---|---|---|---|
| 1968 | 1851 | 1406 | 336 | 109 |
| 1969 | 1978 | 1472 | 390 | 116 |
| 1970 | 2130 | 1624 | 391 | 115 |
| 1971 | 1991 | 1520 | 357 | 113 |
| 1972 | 1739 | 1310 | 306 | 123 |
| 1973 | 1753 | 1333 | 289 | 131 |
| 1974 | 2028 | 1529 | 359 | 140 |
| 1975 | 1745 | 1337 | 303 | 105 |
| 1976 | 1659 | 1298 | 240 | 121 |

*Source*: 'Trade and Industry' (Vol. 29 No. 9, 2 December 1977).

The illustration describes the cycle of a particular invest-ment project. Where the scale and cost of a project is smal (say, less than £25000) some of these stages are often further condensed. The various steps can still be discerned, albeit in an embryo form, and will not be overlooked by good project management. On the other hand, the bigger the project the more explicit, sub-divided and formalised are the various stages likely to be. The three main stages are, of course, sequential, with the output of one stage forming part of the input for the next stage and there may be substantial time gaps between the stages in practice. The process can be stopped at any stage but with increasing costs as it develops.

The plant investment process has a number of important characteristics which influence the effectiveness of its operation:

*Discontinuity*. The plant investment process stops with the successful operation of new equipment. By comparison, the main activities of a manufacturing business such as production and marketing are essentially on-going tasks. Organisation structures and working procedures express their relative permanence. In many firms, especially if they are small, investment in new production plant is a comparatively intermittent, temporary affair. Project procedures tend to reflect this. If they exist at all, they are often *ad hoc* in structure and intended to deal with a specific situation. The 'administrative tooling-up costs' are difficult to justify unless there is a regular stream of project opportunities. The higher frequency of projects where companies have substantial investment programmes encourages the development of standard practices. These tend to concentrate on the manner of project evaluation and submission.

The formation and maintenance of a project team can also be a problem, At its simplest level an operational manager or staff technologist may be given project responsibilities in addition to his regular duties. Such work may be spare-time by nature and correspond to the 'shopping basket' purchase of minor, standard equipment. In these cases no organisational dispositions are required; there is sufficient organisational slack (spare staff capacity) to accommodate such tasks. As we shall see in the next chapter this usually covers only a small part of a firm's capital expenditure.

As soon as the project content requires full-time secondment what happens to the role previously filled by the new project engineer? Will he return to his permanent role when the assignment is completed and where, in that case, should his substitute in that role be placed? Intermittent project work will, therefore, cause periodic organisational adjustments. This can be compounded where the technical background of the project engineer is important; different plant projects could involve different specialists such as a metallurgist for a new plating plant, a paint technologist for a new printing line, etc.

An important benefit of scale is realised when the level of plant investments is sufficient to sustain a permanent project group. Typically, there could be a core team of project staff which is reinforced as required by work load and mix. The problem of discontinuity can be resolved to a large degree. Nevertheless, here too, fluctuations in work load can still cause severe difficulties and companies often go to great lengths to keep project teams together.

| *Stage* | *Input* | *Process* | *Output* |
|---|---|---|---|
| 1<br>Preparation | Stimuli<br>Terms of reference<br>Standard data<br>Staff resources | Proposition<br>Development and Justification | Capital expenditure<br>Proposal 'X' |
| 2<br>Decision | Proposal 'X'<br>Objectives<br>Policies<br>Financial accounts<br>Forecasts | Authorisation<br>Decision | Instructions to proceed with project |
| 3<br>Implementation | Project brief<br>Finance<br>Organisational resources | Design<br>Procurement<br>Construction<br>Commissioning<br>Outcome<br>Evaluation | Effective production plant |

**Figure 6.1** An overall systems concept of the plant investment process

*Division of labour*. Consider any project of substance, such as the extension of a factory or the installation of new production processes. The project could involve such diverse activities as design, plant specification, purchasing, forecasting estimating, costing, site work, plant commissioning, etc. With these come a series of specialists each making decisions in his area of competence. The specialists may be part of the project team or, with lesser schemes, retain membership of corresponding functional departments, *e.g.*, project costing by the factory management accountant. Decisions which are made at detail specialist or operational levels are encapsulated in investment proposals. Unless top managers keep in close touch with project groups their decision can be limited to a yes/no choice of one or a small number of 'homogenised investment proposals'. The division of labour between the preparation/implementation stages and the overall project authorisation decision can have some important consequences. Quite often we get different groups of people ill-aligned with each other. They make different assumptions and work within different information systems. This can lead to the fear by top management that engineers tend to 'gold-plate' their equipment proposals. Engineers, in turn, often feel that the board does not do justice to the needs of effective manufacturing operations. We have partial truths here. The important thing for management, however, is to realise the implications of this natural and necessary work division and to guide the investment process accordingly.

*The need for integration.* Consider further the case of a factory expansion and look at its possible operational implications. Take the ostensibly simple question: How big an increase in capacity shall we have? Immediate derivatives of this question, typically, are:

(i) capital costs,

(ii) economy of scale on capital and revenue accounts,

(iii) expected sales,

(iv) expected contribution,

(v) plant utilisation levels,

(vi) working capital requirements,

(vii) manpower and training requirements, etc.

How are these separate aspects integrated? The project manager—the individual responsible for the task of preparation or implementation, whatever his title in an organisation—will have to harmonise and integrate the different specialist constributions. That task is at the detailed project level. But there needs to be a much deeper integration—at the level of corporate intent. For instance, a given degree of expansion can be interpreted in different or even conflicting ways by various functional managers. The sales manager sees the expansion as an opportunity to challenge an entrenched competitor. The works manager sees the same project as a justification for a new maintenance building. The bigger the project the greater is the need for the integration of intent in terms of corporate plans. Even with smaller projects, such as the replacement of individual machines, the cumulative second-order effects require an overview, an integration.

*Plant investment: the agent of change.* As we shall see in the next chapter, plant investment is a major vehicle of change. It embodies innovation. The changes it may bring can, of course, be far more subtle and complex than the visual impact of new equipment. New plant, even if similar to what it replaces, represents a discontinuity in an operational sense. It impinges on aspirations and fears, gives bargaining opportunities, qualifies existing systems, causes new headaches. These effects are, however, not always pathological. Change will take place eventually in any case, with or without investment except that in the latter case it might be much more uncomfortable. The recognition and utilisation of this association with change will make the overall management of the plant investment process correspondingly more effective.

*The project experience feedback loop.* Figure 6.1 shows the output of the project implementation stage as 'effective production plant'. This is a physical condition where plant performance is related to set criteria. The means of verification is the project audit which will be discussed. The project which has turned out well in all respects is not likely to be the subject of detailed scrutiny. This reflects the principle of management by exception. However, there are plenty of projects which do not reach this level, and their imperfections provide the learning opportunity. The experience can be utilised for future projects; Figure 6.2 illustrates such a notion of experience transfer. The experience may reflect shortcomings in project administration or control, contractual, technical or plant operational problems, in fact every aspect which affects project success. The feedback can be formal in 'inquest' and instruction terms. It may be informal yet still be quite definite, such as a senior manager's resolution never to go to a certain contractor again. The effectiveness of this learning process depends on the formulation of experience (project audit), the management system for capital project work and the ease of information transfer between working groups. Where substantial investment programmes result in a large number of projects, say over 100 a year, there is usually a continuity of comparative projects which facilitates experience transfer to subsequent work. The yield is less where significant projects (over £10000) are only occasional; memories fade and staff change. Again, where a company assigns much of its project work to consultants or 'main contractors' the internal experience yield will also be reduced.

**Plant Investment and the Corporate Intent**

The relationship between plant investment and corporate intent can be most important. This warrants an examination of how the plant investment process fits into the total company system. From this point of view projects can be divided into three categories:

(i) The major strategic project to which the fortunes or even the survival of the company may be hostage.

(ii) The small, relatively routine project covered by regular budget provision, such as the use of depreciation funds for plant replacement. The project itself may not be of great significance at the corporate level.

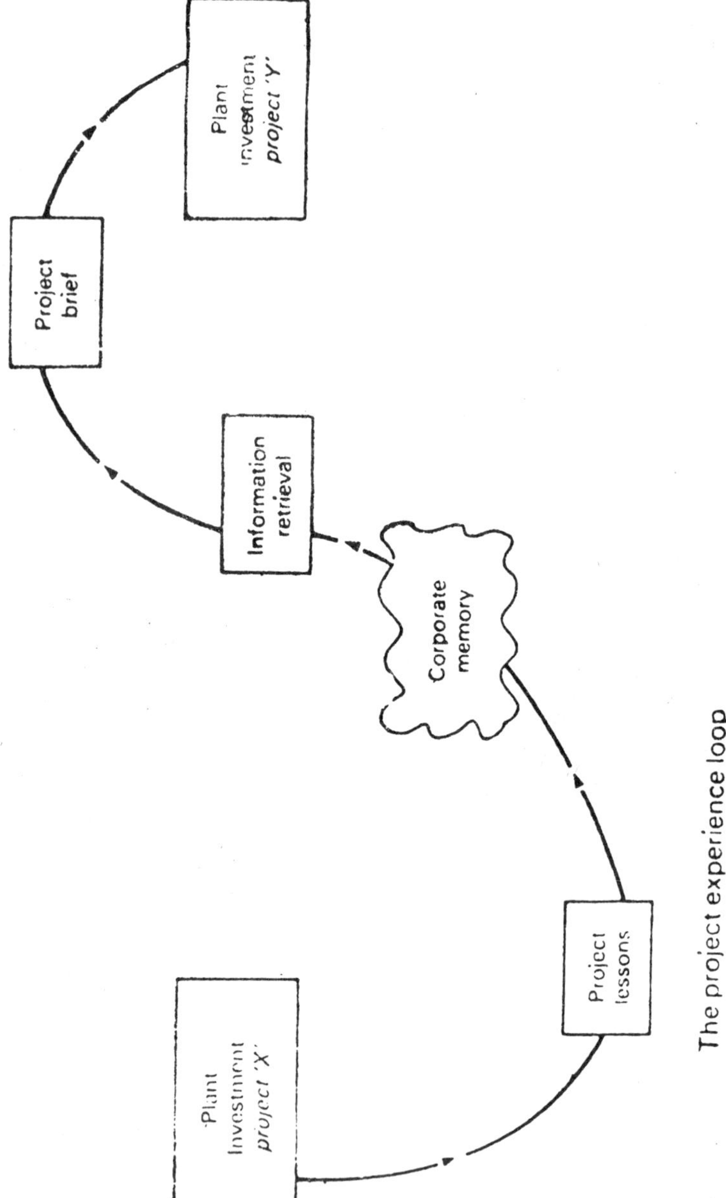


**Figure 6.2** The project experience loop

However, the category or group to which it belongs is important as an expression of company intent.

(iii) The 'conglomerate project' which fits neither of these categories. As a 'special case'—and there are a surprisingly large number of these—it can be the destroyer of systems. (The best way to approach such a project from a management/systems point of view is to divide it into strategic and routine constituents).

What then is meant by the term: corporate intent? It is used here to describe a hierarchy of concepts. At the basic level we are concerned with *business purpose*. This describes the role of the business in relation to the outside world. In an economic sense it is expressed in terms of goods and services offered to meet a known or expected demand. Next, *business objectives* are a set of aims or goals which give a practical expression to the overall statement of purpose. *Strategy* is concerned with the disposition and arrangement of resources to achieve business objectives in a market setting. The definition of objectives and strategies provides the basis for policy development. Urwick's definition of the term 'policy' is perhaps the most comprehensive interpretation:

> *Policy*. This expresses the broad outline of the course it is hoped to pursue and which will govern the detailed action of all who work to the policy. The policy then becomes the governing theory and reappears in a modified form at each level of authority and for each technical function.

Thus, terms of reference are provided for detailed planning, execution and control. Figure 6.3 shows the relationships between the various concepts. It will be noted that such terms as profit maximisation or company long-term survival are not part of the hierarchy. They are hoped-for results, but not as such the vehicle of intent. They reflect motivation and provide both criteria and measuring sticks.

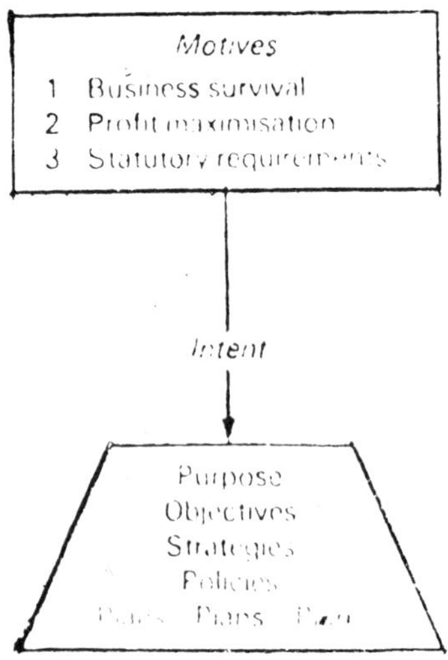


**Figure 6.3** The hierarchy of business intent

The responsibility for spelling out the corporate intent and making it the basis for operation belongs to the 'top management' of the company. This applies particularly to the formulation and authorisation of policies. Top management in the United Kingdom refers primarily to the directors of companies as defined in the Companies Acts. Others may, of course, be involved in the preparation of policies but they would not be formally responsible for their adoption and review.

The expression of intent can best be seen in terms of corporate planning. This puts aside the daily preoccupations of operational management. It is concerned with the long run and how the business should be developed over such a time scale. Typically, this could cover a period of two to ten years. A shorter time scale encounters too many of the constraints of an ongoing business. Beyond ten years the setting usually becomes too tenuous for meaningful planning. This does not negate forecasting for longer ahead as a part of general business intelligence.

Corporate planning starts with the assessment of the business environment and how this might change with time. The environment is seen in economic, political, social and technological terms. The impact of expected changes, their nature and probability, are related to company operations. Thus a number of different scenarios is built up. Each has its structure, promise (plus or minus), likelihood; and to these can be added a proposed response. A portfolio of action alternatives is thus created in terms of established operations as well as new markets, products and processes. In the end a particular set of objectives is chosen and plans formulated for their attainment. It will be appreciated that corporate planning is an overall, integrated activity. It is more than a financial plan or an extrapolition of this year's budget; it embraces all the major functional areas of the business; marketing, manufacture, research and development, personnel and finance. It is concerned with all the resources required by the company to achieve its future objectives. This includes cash, trained personnel, equipment, processes and knowhow. Those who wish to know more about corporate planning are advised to consult such writers as Hertz[2] or Hussey.[3]

### *The Investment Process and Corporate Planning*

The comprehensive nature of corporate planning would be vitiated if the planning of future investment were excluded. This is particularly so where investments call for heavy financial commitment and where years may elapse before the plant comes into operational use—never mind the recovery the initial outlay. Indeed, it is often the exigencies and costs of a proposed investment programme, with all its preconceptions and assumptions, which prompts some managements to look more carefully into the other functional constituents of corporate planning. For instance, a not uncommon experience is one where new production processes, embodied in recently installed equipment, call for a different labour and craft mix from what is currently available. Such a realisation emphasises the development and integration of all forward planning.

There are many links between corporate planning and the plant investment process. Indeed, the latter can be seen as a derivative of the former. There is a correlation between corporate planning and large-scale investment programmes. Both are characteristic of the big international corporation. In overall terms, the relationship between the two is illustrated by Figure 6.4. Simultaneous to the development of markets, products and processes to manufacture, attention is given to the planing of new production facilities. These include all production plant, services, land and buildings required to meet specified capacity targets. The plant investment process is one major form of implementing the corporate plan.

The impingemeni of the corporate plan is in the form of inputs to the three stages of the plant investment process. It begins with opportunity scanning and the whole catchment framework for stimuli, typically, in the Research and Development (R & D) function. It can govern the terms of reference set for project preparation and becomes an ingredient of project evaluation. At the decision stage the investment proposal is related to the corporate intent, which reappears after authorisation in the project brief.

It would be misleading, however, to sugget that corporate planning, whether explicit or intuitive, is the sole actuator of the plant investment process. The stimuli, suggestions and pressures for plant investment can come from many quarters. Promising innovations and developments are not always perceived at the corporate level. Many minor schemes will be sustained by ongoing, delegated resorces provision; but above a given level the corporate intent mustendorse and adopt them.

**Investment and the Organisation Structure**

Consider the number of plant projects authorised by a division of company B (engineering industry) in three successive years: 217, 257, 187; or for a factory of company D (food industry)

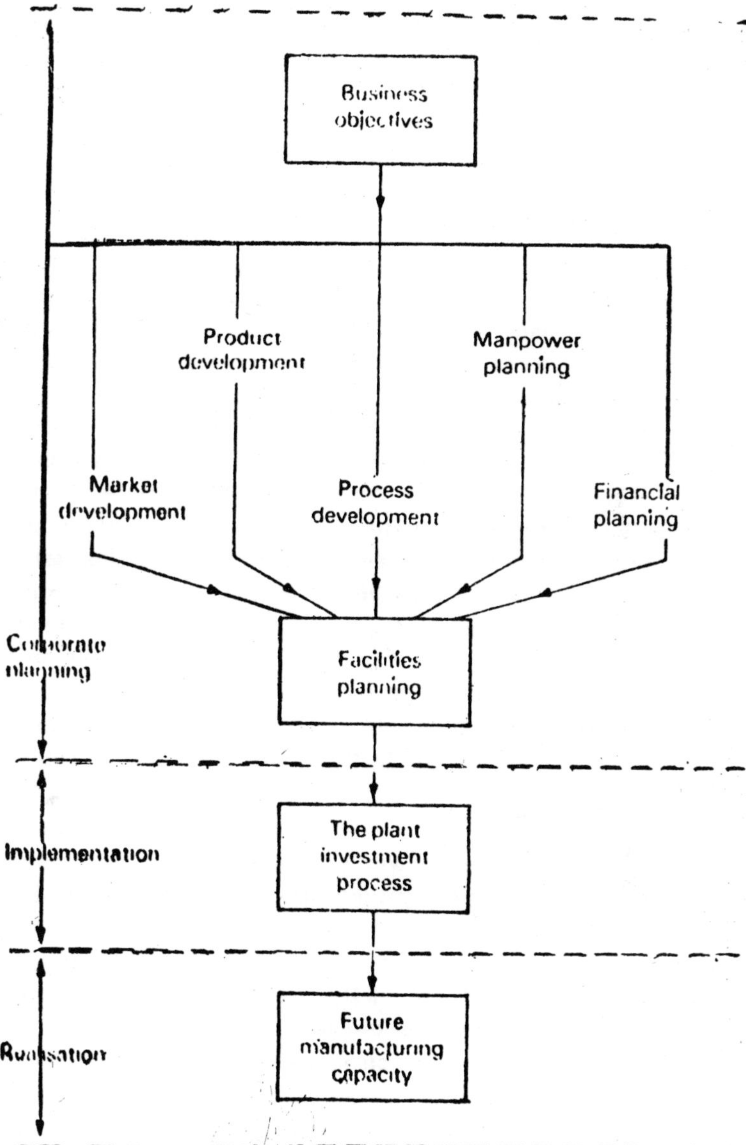


**Figure 6.4.** The plant investment process related to corporate planning.

for the same years: 238, 170, 89. The project value patterns approximate a Paretan distribution, *i.e.*, a small number of projects account for a large percentage of the total investment value. The project numbers are sub-totals and are paralleled by other units in the respective companies. 81 per cent of the projects for company B and 68 per cent of the projects for company D were directly concerned with factory operations.

How should the work content of these projects be structured within a company organisation? The scrutiny of organisation charts—and many firms do not make their organisation explicit—suggests that only a modest number of companies make organisational provision for the preparation and implementation activities of the investment process. Both activities and responsibilities are scattered across the functional organisation. Such a situation is defended by reference to the intermittent and variable nature of investment projects within the company. Even where some organisational provision exists the groups concerned often have other briefs, such as production planning or process development. This understandable. Yet something is lost and what this is can, perhaps, be best described as the initiative responsibility for the plant investment process. Consider Figures 6.5a and 6.5b.Each major function, such as marketing or production, has a senior executive responsible for its results. It is seldom that such a crystallised responsibility exists for a company's capital expenditure programme. Even where a works manager/director has a major involvement, his responsibilities are usually truncated. The differences in organisational treatment reflect some of the characteristics of the plant investment process. For instance, well-defined organisational roles reflect established operations; plant investment, as an agent of change, often runs counter to this. Large, strategic projects also involve other functions, apart from production. Figure 6.5 b also suggests some more-detailed aspects which are often found with small/medium projects. It reflects the typical divison of labour in an engineering firm in terms of routine operational activities. Plant investment stuides do not come into such categories. We are concerned here with an amalgam of technological and economic considerations. One set tends to be dealt with, often in isolation, by engineers; the other is regarded as the usual prerogative of accountants. Such a condominium of functional specialists weakens the responsibility for initiative in plant investment studies. The nature and source of the first stimulus is also a complication here—no one in a manufacturing organisation has a monopoly of ideas which suggests that he be given sole responsibility for their further development into investment proposals. Furthermore there are behavioural implications. Much of the normal

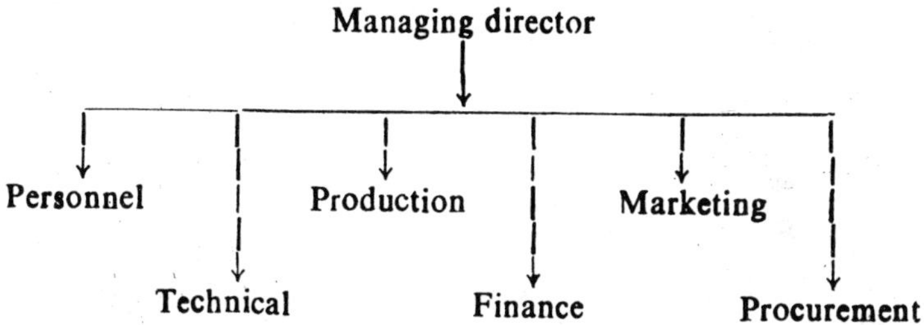


**Figure 6.5 (a)** Main functional divisions of a large engineering group

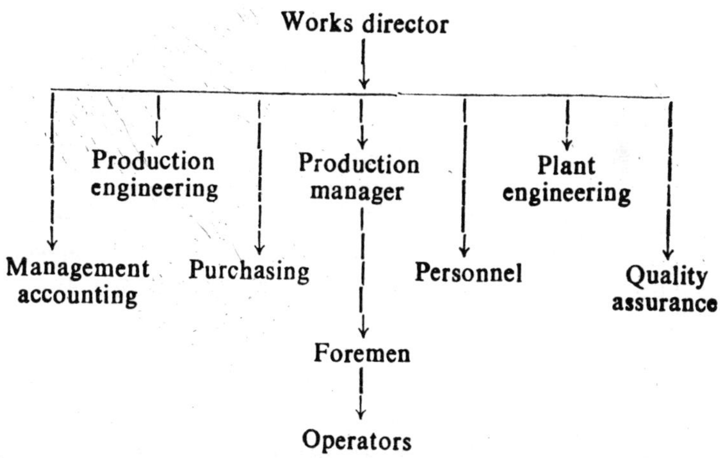


**Figure 6.5 (b)** Main sub-divisions of a typical engineering works organisation

work at technical and supervisory level is of a routine nature. The development of plant proposals has aspects of escape from such a setting; however tenuous at times, there are vistas of new opportunities. there may be more contacts with higher levels of management and outside specialists. These provide opportunities for job satisfaction and other aspirations.

By no means the least of considerations is the control of resources entrusted to those in charge of capital expenditure projects. This applies both to staff and to finance, even if in the latter case cash releases are controlled at board level. Where significant projects are intermittent the quest for control of such resources may run against the concentration of responsibility for plant investment studies.

*Organisational Frameworks for the Plant Investment Process*

Having dwelled no some of the problems relating to the plant investment process, it might be helpful to give some organisational approaches for consistent operations:

*A separate projct/engineering division.* This becomes economic when the scale and continuity of work is assured. Because of this requirement, such an organisation tends to be confined to relatively few large companies with substantial investment budgets. Its head may be a main board director and provide the link with corporate planning (where this exists) and policy levels. Such a divison is normally responsible for most of the preparation and implementation stages of the plant investment process. Its relationships with operating divisions or factories are particularly important as these furnish much of the impetus and input for new projects as well as being in the 'client role.'

*The specialist staff group.* Where plant investment are at a more modest but still significant level a staff group may have special responsibilities for certain stages for the investment process. The role of the group has more of an advisory than an executive content. It reflects a staff function whose main job is to translate proposal from operating divisions into effective plant propositions, but leaving the execution of these to others. In a multi-factory organisation they are often a head office service department. Much of the work is assigned to major contractors and the group tends to become 'in-house' consulting engineers. Unless there are very severe fluctuations of capital expenditure, the group will have a permanent core and a wider membership which can vary by secondment of the appropriate specialists from, say, R & D or operating departments. If there is considerable variation in the type or size of individual projects then organisational flexibility will become important. Staff may be structured in a form of matrix organisation where they participate in an interdisciplinary project team, answerable to a project manager, yet still are responsible for specialist work to a specialist head of department. The nature and implications of such organisation structures have been well documented by such writers as Knight.[4]

*Direct line management responsibility.* This approach can be found where much of a company's capital expenditure is composed of small to medium sized projects (say, up to £100000). In essence, the line manager responsible for the effectiveness of his department or works would also be responsible for the preparation and submission of investment proposals designed to improve its operations. He would be assisted by appropriate staff within his authority to whom the bulk of such tasks would be delegated. However, his responsibility would remain unabrogated. In a sense, he is both line and project manager.

Company A, for instance, regarded the formulation and handling of such matters as an aspect of managerial competence. It wanted its line managers to be involved and committed to project undertakings. They were also responsible for project execution, within authorised resources and a defined span of discretion. Line management involement and responsibility for project preparation was seen to be fundamental, because those very same managers were subsequently expected to achieve the project intentions.

## REFERENCES

1. Urwick, L., *Elements of Administration*, Pitman, (London 1947)

2. Hertz, D.B., *New Power for Management*, McGraw-Hill (New York, 1969),

3. Hussey, D:E., *Introducing Corporate Planning*, Pergamon Press. (Oxford, 1971).

4. Knight, K. *Matrix Management*, Gower, Press, (Farnborough Hants, 1977).

# 7

# PROGRESS MEASUREMENT DURING PROJECT EXECUTION

M. P. BUDDHDEO
S. K. GUPTA*

Progres measurement in project organisations has always been a riddle for project managers. The Measurement of progress in design work, material procurement and construction activity is one of the most important and difficult activities in project management. Accurate measurement of such work is pre-requisite for successful completion of a project. This help in setting the realistic targets. The measurement of progress on a regular basis (weekly/monthly/ quarterly, etc.) identifies the phases of the project in which the progress is slow and force the management to analyse the underlying reasons for the slow progress. This provides signals and clues to take corrective action whenever the actual progress is lagging behind the planned progress on a particular date. It has been observed a number of times that no systematic approach is followed in

*Mr. M.P. Buddhdeo is Senior Engineer, Engineers India Ltd., New Delhi.
Dr. S.K. Gupta is Visiting Associate Professor, University of North Carolina, Department of Business Administration, Greensboro USA.

the measurement of the progresss in the project work. Generally the estimates are made and the targets are set based on past experience which prove only a rough and unsatisfactory guideline. This makes the persons who are supposed to monitor the progress of the project ineffective. The point that the lack of an effective method for project measurement leads to delays in project completion has been highlighted during a symposium organised by the Project Management Association in 1980. Progress measurement has been identified as one of the potential and critical areas of research in project management. Knowledge in this field is of great strategic value and can be most helpful in the formulation of project policy. Without measurement in this area (even of a veey crude kind), project policy would have to be based on a priori estimates and untested hunches. The objective of the present paper is to provide a method to measure the progress during different phases of project life.

*Current Practices*

A project has to pass through various stages before completion. The three major phases of the project life may be identified as:

—Design and Engineering phase

—Procurement of Material/Equipment phase

—Construction phase

The current practices of measuring the progress may vary from firm to firm. However, some of the common methods are:

(i) Design and Engineering phase:

Percentage progress

$$= \frac{\text{Actual man hours spent as on date}}{\text{Estimated man hours}} \times 100$$

(ii) Procurement phase: Measurement can be done either on the basis of value or efforts spent.

$$\text{Percentage progresson value basis} = \frac{\text{Value of material received on site as on date}}{\text{Total value of material to be purchased}} \times 100$$

$$\text{Percentage progress on efforts basis} = \frac{\text{Man hours spent as on date}}{\text{Estimated procurement man hours}} \times 100$$

These two methods may give different results.

(iii) Construction phase: Measurement of progress in construction phase is generally done on the basis of man hours/efforts spent as in the above phases. However, the following types of statements are also made while reporting the progress of work: "So and so foundation is completed; tower X is erected; piping of 1 km has been laid; and so on." Such statements do not give any idea about the actual progress made.

The inherent defect in these practices is that it does not bring to surface the inefficiency in carrying out the work because it shows X per cent of progress if X per cent of man hours/efforts have been spent whereas the corresponding physical progress may not have been made.

*Conceptual Framework of Progress Measurement*

The fundamental concept of progress measurement in this paper is to stress upon the physical progress rather than the efforts or money actually spent. It is achieved by dividing the total scope of the work into measurable activities. Each activity is further divided into job steps Each of step has certain pre-determined percentage progress which is awarded when the job step is completed. When all the job steps of an activity are completed it is considered that the activity is 100 per cent complete.

Further, in a project generally there are several items (requiring same set of job steps) in one particular type of activity. Since all the items need not necessarily require same total efforts, it is suggested to introduce weightage factor for calculating the overall progress. The overall progress can be calculated for a department, or for total engineering work (covering all the departments) or for the entire project. The weightage factors can be decided based upon the man hours required for each activity.

This conceptual framework is represented with the help of Figure 7.I.

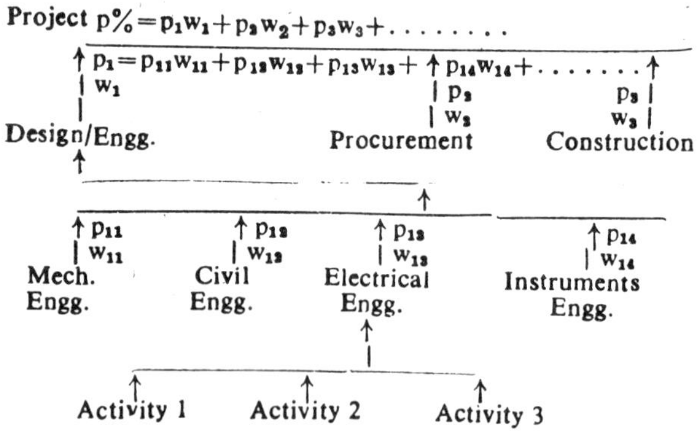


| Job Steps | Job Steps | Job Steps |
|---|---|---|
| 1 | 1 | 1 |
| 2 | 2 | 2 |
| 3 | 3 | 3 |
| 4 | 4 | 4 |
| 5 | 5 | 5 |
| .. | .. | .. |
| .. | .. | .. |
| .. | .. | .. |

**Fig. 7.1**

The progress of the project on a given date will depend upon the progress made in the various phases comprising the project. The figure showns that the project will be completed when three phases of the project, *viz.*, design/engineering, procurement and construction are completed.

The percentage progress 'p' of the project may be represented by the following formula:

$p=p_1w_1+p_2w_2+p_3w_3$, where $p_1$, $p_2$ and $p_3$ are the percentage progress made in each phase and $w_1$, $w_2$ and $w_3$ are the weights assigned to each phase. In general, if there are n phases of a project, then $p=\sum_{i=1}^{n} pi\ wi$, where $\sum_{i=1}^{n} wi=1$.

The progress pi of ith phase may be calculated in a similar manner, that is,

$$pi=\sum_{j=1}^{mi} pij.\ wij,\ i=1,2\ldots\ldots\ldots\ldots,n \text{ and}$$

mi is the number of sub-phases of phase i, pij and wij are the progress made and weight assigned to jth sub-phase of phase i, $(j=1, 2.\ldots\ldots\ldots mi)$, $\sum_{j=1}^{mi} wij=1$.

Such calculations continue till we reach the activity level. Each activity comprises several job steps which are to be performed in a sequence. The progress of each activity depends on the job steps completed for that activity. The next section outlines a method to assign percentage progress to each job step.

*Method for Assigning Percentage Progress*

The steps followed in setting up the percentages, for each job step milestone are as follows:

(i) Divide the activities into the job steps/milestone.

(ii) Select representative items of the acticity with estimated man-hours to complete each one of them.

(iii) Estimated man-hours of each representative item are further broken into man-hours for each job step/ milestone.

(iv) The percentage progress represented by each job step is set equal to the percentage of man-hours (taking into account all the representative means) represented by that job step. This is rounded to the nearest multiple of 5, because this much accuracy is sufficient keeping in view the fact that only representative items have been selected out of many and the calculations are to be done for a large number of activities.

*Example*

To illustrate this concept consider the material requisition activity of a mechanical engineering department, equipments:

Step (i) The various job steps/milestones are:

—Prepare and issue material requisition to purchase department for enquiry.

—Bids evaluation and prepare technical recommendation to client.

—Prepare and issue purchase requisition after incorporating comments of client.

—Vendor print checking.

—Finalise engineering requirement.

Step (ii) The following four items are selected with their estimated man-hours:

| | |
|---|---|
| (A) Dryer feed pump | 40 man-hours |
| (B) Process air compressor | 350 man-hours |
| (C) Bottom pump for a column | 40 man-hours |
| (D) Agitator | 70 man-hours |

Steps (iii) and (iv) are represented in Table 7.1;

TABLE 7.1

| *Job Steps* | *Man hours required for selected items* | | | | *Total for a'l items (hrs.)* | ***Man hours* (%)** | *Suggested progress (rounded to nearest 5%)* | *Cumulative progress (%)* |
|---|---|---|---|---|---|---|---|---|
| | *A* | *B* | *C* | *D* | | | | |
| | *1* | *2* | *3* | *4* | *5* | *6* | *7* | *8* |
| Prepare and issue material requisition for enquiry | 8 | 60 | 10 | 15 | 93 | 18.6 | 20 | 20 |
| Bids evaluation and prepare technical recommendations | 15 | 100 | 13 | 20 | 148 | 29.6 | 30 | 50 |
| Prepare and issue purchase requisition | 10 | 65 | 10 | 15 | 100 | 20.0 | 20 | 70 |
| Vendor print checking | 2 | 90 | 2 | 15 | 109 | 21.8 | 20 | 90 |
| Finalisation of engineering requirements | 5 | 35 | 5 | 5 | 50 | 10.0 | 10 | 100 |
| Total | 40 | 350 | 40 | 70 | 500 | — | — | — |

*Method for Measuring Progress*

Once the percentage progress represented by each job-step/ milestone has been determined, the progress of a project can be measured on any particular rate by accumulating the progress made on each item of each activity of the project as given below:

Consider the same actitivity as before, *i.e.*, material equisitioning activity in a small project and suppose there are 5 pumps to be purchased. Purchase of each pump represents an item in this activity and the total time required for the purchase of each pump may be different. The status of these pumps, *i.e.*, the job steps completed as on a particular data is give below in Table 7.2.

TABLE 7.2

| *Pump No.* | *Estimated manhours to complete the total work* | *Weight* | *Status as on date (job step completed)* | *% Progress* |
|---|---|---|---|---|
| 1 | 50 | .167 | Material requisitions issued for enquiry | 20 |
| | 75 | .250 | Bids evaluated | 50 |
| 3 | 100 | .333 | Vendor print checking done | 90 |
| 4 | 50 | .167 | Engineering requirements finalised. | 100 |
| 5 | 25 | .083 | Material requisitions issued for enquiry | 20 |
| Total | 300 Hrs. | 1.00 | | |

The method suggested in this paper to calculate the overall progress is to weigh the progress made for each pump. The weight assigned to a pump is its estimated man-hours divided by total manhours.

%progress=2(x°167+50x°250+90x°333+100x°167=20x°.083
=65.17%

Suppose 250 manhours have been spent on this job so far, then according to the current practice, the progress would be reported as 83.3 per cent $\left(\frac{250}{300}\times 100\right)$ as against 64.17 per cent calculated by the proposed method. If actual manhours spent are only 150, then the reported progress would be 50 per cent. Thus the existing method suffers from the inherent defect of under estimating/over-estimating the progress made because it does not take into account the actual physical progress made.

*Conclusions*

The current practices in progress measurement in project work specially in design and procurement of materials do not always lead to correct assessment of the progress because efficiency is totally ignored. The system proposed in this paper awards progress at the completion of job steps/milestones which are physically measurable. The method requires technical knowledge on the part of those persons who are monitoring the progress of the project. This method has the following major advantages:

—Efficiency of the people involved in the system is considered.

—In every time period (week, month, etc,) the progress to be achieved can be scheduled in such a way that total project is finished in the targeted period.

—The progress of the work can be checked at any time by a third party, if necessary.

# 8

# PROJECT EVALUATION

The basic project preparation task leads to a defined project proposal. Two of the most important constituents of the proposal development task are the computation of capital expenditure and the expected project benefits. The job of project evaluation is to relate these two estimates, *i.e.* to establish the worth of the project in financial terms. Most of the chapter will be devoted to this form of evaluation but before doing so let us see project evaluation in perspective.

As evaluation only has meaning when there is something tangible to consider, a proposal must be formulated first. Evaluation need not, however, wait until the preparation task is complete particularly where preparation costs are considerable. Two of the main decision stages of the preparation process include a form of evaluation, however tentative that might be. One can see evaluation at several levels, each with organisational and systems implications:

*The strategic and policy level.* This assesses the relevance of the investment proposal in relation to company objectives and policies. Such evaluation may be carried out by a board committee or in large corporations by a corporate planning department. Plant investment project at this level may be concerned with major extensions, the building of new factories or basic changes in production processes. The evaluation would obviously take place at an early stage of project formulation.

*The implementation evaluation level.* This level presumes the proposal relevance but examines every aspect of intent. It is concerned with operating statements, financial commitments and expectations, forecasts and all claims made by the project preparation group or sponsoring management. The biggest opportunity here is to question the assumptions on which the case for an investment rests. Project alternatives may be proposed and considered with the purpose of optimising the worth of a proposition. Risk analysis and financial evaluation techniques may also be applied. This level of evaluation is applicable to all plant projects of substance where there is an element of novelty or uncertainty. Much of such an evaluation may be carried out explicity or intuitively by a senior line manager, with or without the help of a personal assistant or someone specially seconded for such purpose. In large companies this form of evaluation is often the responsibility of a management services group.

*The financial evaluation level.* This level accepts the soundr ness of the operating and technical premises of the proposition for which others take the responsibility. It is confined to the direct assessment of the project financial data, particularly the claimed benefits, or, alternatively, verifies the financial statements prepared by the project preparation group or project sponsors. This evaluation is usually carried out by the accounting function, or, where the scale, importance or the politics of the project warrant it, by consulting accountants. Typically, the company auditors may be retained for such a purpose.

The classification of different evaluation levels is a helpful concept although in practice one can expect some overlap. The distinction between the project preparers and evaluators may be reinforced by the organisational framework, for instance where the preparers are at factory level and the evaluators are attached to head office. But in the absence of such framework, particularly with the medium to small firm, this distinction may be blurred. Even on the time scale of preparation and evaluation there may be some overlap. Where a complex project requires extensive preparation work, some evaluation tasks may begin on completed sections, before the whole project is finalised in detail.

With our concentration on financial evaluation it is helpful to remember that projects with non-economic objectives or non-quantifiable benefits are not amenable to this form of anlysis—although some forms of cost-benefit assessment might be applied. Typically, two forms of project benefit cannot be properly judged on financial criteria: (i) *Social welfare benefits*. For example, a company may undertake substantial capital expenditures on a new works canteen, employee amenities or to bring the factory in line with the requirements of the Health and Safety at Work Act 1974. (ii) *Functional benefits*. The benefits can be perceived but are difficult to measure. Thus an investment can result in a better company reputation, more customer goodwill, etc. Its precise impact on the company's financial performance is, however, hard to define.

## The Background to Evaluation

This section will consider some of the background factors which influence the financial evaluation of a project. Whilst some of these factors might not become explicit it is seldom that an evaluation is carried out in a 'vacuum'.

### *Capital Expenditure Forecasts*

These are usually long term by nature, typically for a period of 2-5 years. The extent to which companies make long-term forecasts of capital expenditure is, generally speaking, a function of their overall long-term planning activity. The systematic development of such forecasts was most noticeable with company B. Within the framework of its five-year sales forecast it was standard practice to prepare a three-year forecast of new capital expenditure, together with an approximate cash outflow profile. Such forecasts at group level were built up from individual factory requirements.

Again, the intent of company C was explicit. Its policy statement on the control of capital expenditure indicated: 'It is a future objective that Managers will also estimate major items required for the four years following the above budget year under review. This section will be implemented when the overall Company long-term plan has been developed.'

*Annual Capital Expenditure Budgets*

These are, of course, an integral part of the basic system of budgetary control and thus subject to the general discipline of specified and timetabled submission, modification and approval. Capital expenditure intentions are thus evaluated and integrated within the company's trading prospect and overall cash flow. The capital expenditure budget is normally divided into land and buildings, plant and machinery and other categories.

Understandably, the amount budgeted for capital xpenditure each year is affected by a number of consideratio First and foremost is the company's trading position and its general financial state, particularly its liquidity and ability to obtain the required capital at the prevailing rates of interest. Secondly, the annual budget may express the implementation of long-term plans. From an operational point of view the company be guided by past experience; for instance, it may set aside a certain part will also of its depreciation cash flow for replacement and modernisation. Apart from these general considerations a number of prepared and evaluated projects may wait, provisionally approved, for inclusion in the next budget.

The actual administration of the capital expenditure budget can vary considerably. Where we have the specific and evaluated project the budget inclusion is tantamount to authorisation.

But much of the budget can remain a general provision for which a particular claim has to be made without any prior guarantee of authorisation. The budget expresses, in essence, the constraint of the capital rationing situation. This applies particularly to minor expenditures within the discretion of line mangement.

It is not, however, necessary for every project to be ear-marked or provided for by a budget. But then it has to be sufficiently attractive or necessary to be considered as an extra-budget claim.

### *Plant Depreciation Policies*

A company's depreciation policy is, of course, a significant parameter in its investment evaluation. Its view on the depreciation rate to be adopted determines plant life in accounting terms. The end of such life terminates the stream of benefits which the calculation can take into account. The physical and operating characteristics of the plant after its notional demise in terms of book value is a separate matter. The DCF calculation is thus affected by a time scale cut-off point, while the return on capital computation is in any case affected by the specific provision for depreciation from the gross benefit.

### *Government Fiscal Measures*

It is common knowledge that government actions affect project decisions. They can also influence the pattern of project evaluation. They affect projects either by providing an incentive, such as regional investment grants, or as a discouragement, such as an increase in corporation tax. One can also distinguish between direct and indirect effects.

The rate of taxation on the generated benefit is of course a key factor in the evaluation of the net project yield and the corresponding cash flow. Similarly, tax allowances can have a major effect on computations. Project evaluation can be on a gross' or 'net of tax' basis. There is a strong case for the 'net' approach, particularly where the project sponsor or preparation group has to make the first evaluation. Taxation, it is argued, is a regrettable fact of life and an appraisal which ignores it is unrealistic. Nevertheless, some companies prefer to view propositions 'gross' rather than 'net'. A company's tax liability is hostage to many other considerations. Many capital projects are for modest or relatively small amounts, taxable profits are uncertain and there is much to be gained from a simple, consistent system freed from the variability of government fiscal measures. Taxation can be allowed for globally by specifying higher cut-off rates. The occational large, strategic project warrants special treatment anyway, but the other, say, 98 per cent of projects would gain from simplification.

As related policy aspects, which is considerably affected by fiscal measures, is the treatment of certain research and development expenditures. If these are capitalised they can have a significant influence on project values and returns.

## The Data for Evaluation

Investment appraisal relates the prospective capital expenditure to the future cash flow it generates. It follows from this that most of the data to be fed into the appraisal task concern these two categories. They are a function of the proposal itself. The unit of account is money, expressed against a time scale. Apart from this there is a special type of information which, for the want of a better term, we can call the parameters of calculation. These reflect the standard practice of the company, *e.g.*, the depreciation or the discount rates to be used.

### *The Required Capital Expenditure*

This statement is usually divided into two categories: the expenditure on fixed assets and the required additional working capital. In the context of investment in production plant the fixed assets normally account for the greater part of the expenditure. However, it need not be so. For instance, a new product may only need one or two extra machines, while the remainder of its production route uses existing equipment. The greater part of the investment may then be to finance the expected sales volume. It is also possible for either category to have a negative value, *i.e.*, to give rise to some disinvestment. This can be quite common where new equipment improves a production process and permits the reduction of work in progress or inventories. Again, it is possible to have an investment project involving a reduction in fixed assets, but except for certain lease-back operations, these are very infrequent and may be ignored here.

Considering first the expenditure on fixed assets, the statement represents a definitive estimate for the purpose of authorisation. Depending on the nature of the work or the type of plant involved it may be accurate io within ±5-10 per cent. The following are the main categories of expense for major projects. For more modest schemes only some of the categories will apply. Each category is also capable of further subdivision.

*Expenditure on Fixed Assets*

1. Site acquisition *A*costs.
2. Acquisition expenses.
3. Site clearance and preparation.
4. Buildings. Erection and alterations.
5. Plant and building services.
6. Plant foundations.
7. Machinery and process plant. This includes associated costs, such as freight, insurance or duty.
8. Plant process and services connections.
9. Installation and erection costs.
10. Tools and fixtures.

11. Personnel, welfare and administrative facilities.
12. Capitalised research and expenditure costs.
13. Design costs.
14. Project management costs.
15. Professional fees.
16. General site costs.
17. Know-how or lump-sum licence payments.

From the overall total fixed assets costs the disposal proceeds of existing redundant plant are deducted. If such disposal proceeds have a time lag these can be discounted to the period of receipt.

*Changes in Working Capital*

1. Inventory levels.
2. Work-in-progress values.
3. Debtors.
4. Creditors.

The estimated salvage value of the project assets at the end of the plant life are treated as a specific receipt accruing in the year of disposal. However, where extended plant life is presumed and the proceeds are likely to be small and uncertain, such salvage values may be neglected, Again, the partial or complete recovery of working capital at the end of operations is treated as a receipt at that time.

*The Definition of Project Benefits*

In this context we are concerned with investment in production plant which is justified on economic grounds. Other, less tangible benefits may also emerge, but these are disregarded for our purpose. Where, then, are the likely sources of these benefits?

In our analysis we are only concerned with identifiable, incremental changes in costs and incomes; *i.e.*, the net effect the project has on the company's cash flow. 'Notional' cash flows and overhead apportionment assumptions are irrelevant to the analysis. The project benefits may be derived from operating financial data under two broad headings:

*Changes in revenue.* Typically these could be due to:

1. An increase in the net effective sales volume, assuming constant prices. The net contribution from the extra sales would constitute the change in cash flow.
2. Higher sales receipts without major changes in volume. Examples of this are premium quality payments, or the reduction in 'seconds'.
3. Any mixture of (1) and (2).
4. Patent, royalty or licensing income.

*Changes in costs.* Many categories of operating costs could be affected by a project. The following are the most important:

1. Direct labour costs of production, including terminal costs for redundancies, etc.
2. Indirect labour and staff costs.
3. Overtime payments (non-productive overtime cost element).
4. Maintenance charges.
5. Plant services: power, gas, air, etc.
6. Tooling, where treated as a revenue charge.
7. Materials. Direct production materials and indirect materials, such as catalysts, refrigerants, lubricants, etc.
8. Consumables.
9. Scrap and rectification charges.

10. Insurances, rates, rent.
11. Transport costs.
12. Stock carrying charges.
13. Finance charges, *e.g.*, in respect of working capital such as work in progress, debtors.
14. Sub-contracting charges.

In many instances the evaluation involves the balancing of savings under some headings against additional costs in other categories. The resultant net figure constitutes the gross project benefit. It is axiomatic that the relevant cost data should be of sufficient accuracy so as not to vitiate the meaning of the investment evaluation which makes use of it. There is little point in evaluation refinement when the source data is rough.

### The Basic Appraisal Techniques

There are moments when the brilliant (or lucky) manager can perceive in a flash the worth of a proposition and without calculation proceeds with the correct action. Lesser mortals have to do their homework. For this purpose some well-established appraisal techniques are available. There is a family name for each major type; within it, are a number of variants. The main techniques are as follows:

(a) The payback method.

(b) The return on investment analysis.

(c) The discounted cash flow technique (DCF),

Before considering the details and respective merits of these techniques it would be helpful if we made explicit some of the principles underlying investment appraisal.

The first principle is the *recovery of the investment.* Whatever the initial yield, the ultimate realisation of the investment is essential. The project must at least generate its own depreciation cash flow. The second is one of *adequacy* of *yield*, considering a firm's total business situation. This subsumes such aspects as the cost of finance to the firm and the risks it is willing to take. The third is the *time value of money*. This principle has not had full attention in the past but with high interest and inflation rates it cannot be disregarded. Only the DCF method incorporates this third principle.

*The Payback Method*

The concept of this method is simple: it measures the time which elapses after the initial capital outlay until the cash flow of generated benefits equals the original investment. Graphically it can be shown as in Figure 8.1.

The general case is as follows:

If E=the project capital expenditure and $R_i$=the project benefit in the 'i' th period, then the payback period is determined by the value of t which solves the equation

$$E = \sum_{i=0}^{i=t} R_i$$

The symbol Σ is the Greek capital letter called sigma. It means here 'the sum of'. In our case it denotes the sum of all the benefits from the moment we start—zero time—untill the 't' the period.

The economic acceptability of a project is then dependent on whether this established value of t is more or less than a prescribed time period T.

Consider a simple example:

| | |
|---|---|
| Capital cost of new machine | £10000 |
| Resultant annual savings | 5000 |

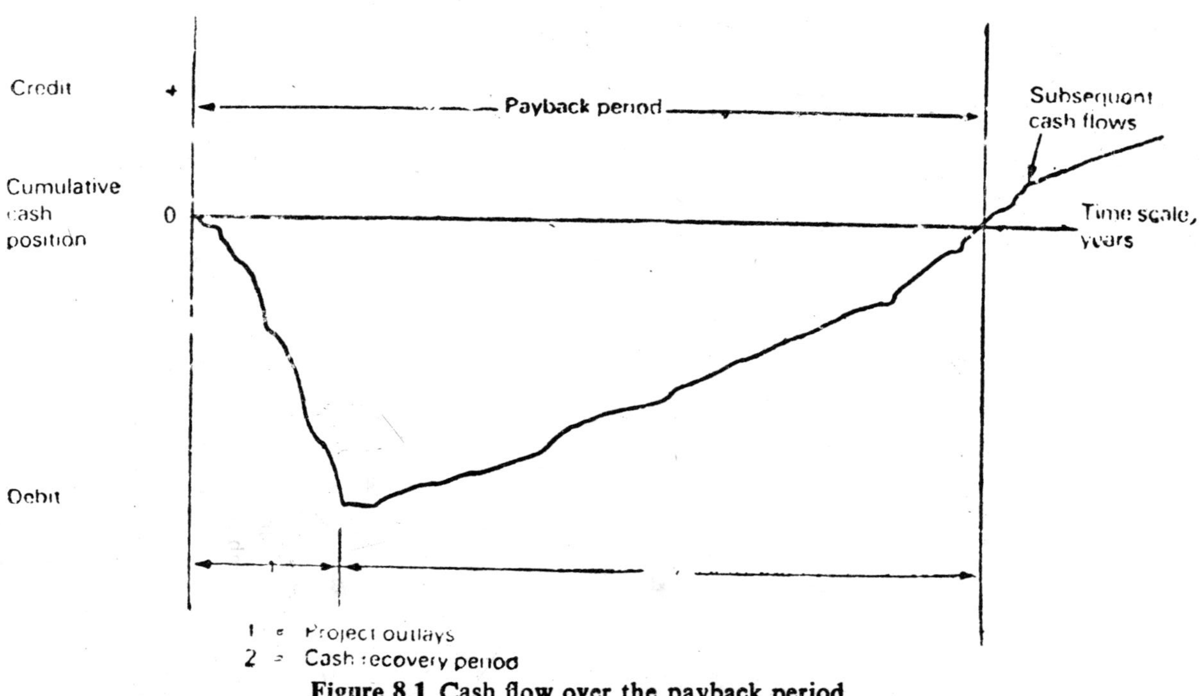


**Figure 8.1 Cash flow over the payback period**

In cash flow terms this means that the outlay will be recovered over two years—the payback period. Assuming now that the company operates at a profit and we have, say:

| | |
|---|---|
| Corporation tax | 50% |
| First year allowance | 100% |

The cash outflow due to the investment is taken to be instantaneous, it occurs in year 0. The cash inflow for year one will have two constituents. First there will be a tax saving of £5000 because the whole of the investment can be deducted from taxable profit. The second part will be the generated benefit of £5000 on which the company will have to pay corporation tax at 50 per cent reducing that cash flow constituent to £2500. Again, after two years the outstanding balance will be cleared, this time by a composition of tax saving and taxed benefits. If the tax on generated benefits is paid in the following tax year the cash recovery is already after twelve months provided the lagged tax payment is covered by savings in year two.

If the specified recovery period for a project is two years then obviously this proposition will be acceptable.

We have a simple, but rather crude, method here. No allowance is made for the timing of proceeds, nor is any note taken of the cash flow after the payback period. The method is inadequate for systematic comparison and rigorous analysis. Its conceptual simplicity is not an advantage if it discourages a more thorough enquiry; its usefulness is more at the initial feasibility appraisal. It is sometimes also used as a short-cut check for minor operational proposals. In such cases there may already be strong technological arguments and the economic seems so overwhelming that no refined calculation is needed.

There is a valuable aspect to the payback graph shown in Figure 8.1. The total area below the zero line is a function of time and money. Multiplying this area by an interest rate will give the financial cost of the committed money. Thus, if the average amount outstanding were, say, £10000 and the payback period five years, then the interest cost over the payback period at 10 per cent would be $1000 \times 5 \times 0.1 = £5000$. This type of evaluation can be salutary to engineers and managers responsible for the detailed dispositions of a plant project. Other things equal, the ordering, installation, commissioning and running of production plant should minimise the below the line area.

*The Return on Investment Analysis*

The horizon is now the expected plant life, not the payback period which may be only a modest fraction of the former. The return on investment method measures in percentage terms the benefit for period 'i' against the original investment. In general, we take the rate of return for year 'i' to be $r_i$

$$\text{where } r_i = \frac{R_i}{E} \, 100\%$$

Taking our previous example and using the simplest form of measurement, the return on capital will be

$$\frac{\text{Annual Saving}}{\text{Investment}} \times 100\% = \frac{5000 \times 100\%}{10000} = 50\%$$

Where the returns vary over the life of the plant 'T' we obtain an average rate of return $r_a$ where

$$r_a = \frac{100}{T} \left( \sum_{i=0}^{i=t} r_i \right) \% = \frac{100}{T} \left( \sum_{i=0}^{i=t} \frac{R_i}{E} \right) \%$$

For instance, if our machine had a working life of four years and its returns for years one, two, three and four were 40 per cent, 50 per cent, 60 per cent and 70 per cent respectively, the average rate of return would come to 55 per cent. The rate of return can be measured gross or net of depreciation. If there were no allowance for depreciation this would presume an infinite machine life. Such an assumption would, of course, be untenable. When we come to plant replacement, the economic life of a machine is not only affected by its deterioration in use but also by competitive technical developments. It is not very easy to make a precise forecast of machine life. A conservative estimate tends to keep it on the short side; a thin proposition may survive with an extended life span. It is important here that a company establishes a standard life forecast practice based on equipment categories of which it has had adequate experience.

Take, for instance, two alternative life spans for our machine: first two years, then five years. Further, assume straight-line depreciation and no equipment salvage value at the end of its working life. On that basis, with a two-year life' the provision for depreciation would have to be £5000 per annum to recover the investment. As a result the generated annual savings of £5000 would reduce to zero after depreciation, *i.e.*, there is no return on the investment. For a five-year period we need to put aside £2000 per annum, leaving an after-depreciation benefit of £3000 per annum. This corresponds to a 30 per cent return on the initial investment. A change in the expected epuipment life forecast can thus be a major influence on project attractiveness.

So far, rates of return have been related to the initial investment. However, the accumulation of depreciation funds means the recovery of the investment with time. The after-depreciation project benefits could then more usefully be related to the outstanding sum. If the benefits remain constant this will have a gratifying effect on the rates of return. Another alternative would to be use the mean asset book value for the whole of the equipment life. Consider again our machine with a five-year life. (See Table 8.1). If a mean book value of £ 6000 were taken, then the rate of return over the five years would be 50 per cent. Year six shows the situation if the equipment survives its book life and continues to make the

TABLE 8.1

| *Year* | *1* | *2* | *3* | *4* | *5* | *6* |
|---|---|---|---|---|---|---|
| Saving (£) | 5000 | 5000 | 5000 | 5000 | 5000 | 5000 |
| Depreciation (£) | 2000 | 2000 | 2000 | 2000 | 2000 | 0 |
| Book value of machine (£) | 10000 | 8000 | 6000 | 4000 | 2000 | 0 |
| Benefit after Depreciation (£) | 3000 | 3000 | 3000 | 3000 | 3000 | 5000 |
| Return on book value (%) | 30 | 37.5 | 50 | 75 | 150 | Infinity |

same savings. From an accounting point of view there is a strong temptation to keep the plant going for ever!

Again, the computation can be further refined in the context of profitable operations by allowing for the appropriate rate corporation tax and initial allowance.

Generally speaking, the basic method has the advantage of easy comparison with the returns of financial investment. It can be readily related to the yield of quoted company shares or the interest rate on borrowed money. There is still no provision, however, for the time element of money. Despite such a limitation this form of analysis is widely used.

*The Discounted Cash Flow (DCF) Technique*

The concept of discounted cash flow has long been associated with banking and insurance calculations, whenever the passage of time and the use of money over such periods was involved. In essence, the concept is concerned with the flow of money in terms of amounts and timing. It allows, in the form of compound interest, for the time-lag between the actual disbursements and the consequent receipts. It permits, with the use of present value tables, the collation of all cash flows irrespective of direction and incidence. In this manner a valid comparison between *capital* expenditure now and subsequent *revenue* benefits can be established.

There are a number of different application of the basic DCF technique, but before describing these in detail it would help to introduce the concept of present value. Imagine you had a deposit of £ 10C with a bank or building society and that you obtained an interest payment of 10 per cent at the end of each year of deposit. As a result the sum of principal and interest would amount to £ 110 at the end of year one and it would further compound to £ 121 at the end of year two, etc. The general case can be expressed by the formula:

$$X=A(1+r)^n$$

where X = amount accumulated

A = principal sum to start with

r = rate of interest

n = number of years of accumulation

Taking our particular illustration for year two we have

$$£121=100(1+0.10)^2$$

This, in substance, is the effect of compounding which makes a given sum today worth more at some future date. Discounting is the opposite process; it takes a given sum at a future date and expresses it at today's value. Thus, the sum of £ 121 in two year's time is worth less at this moment. Taking the same interest rate and time span of our previous example we come back to our original deposit of £ 100. Instead of multiplying by $(1+0\ 10)^2$ we divide by this amount. The general relationship is given by

$$Y=\frac{B}{(1+r)^n}$$

where B = a cash flow in year 'n'

Y = the present value of that cash flow, given a rate of interest 'r'

for all positive values of 'n', *i.e.*, the future, the expression

$$\frac{1}{(1+r)^n}$$

is less than one. This expression is known as the discount factor. In our illustration, when $r=0.10$ and $n=2$, its value is 0.826. It will be noted that the higher the rate of interest, also known as the rate of discount, the lower will be the discount factors. Again, as 'n' increases the factor values diminish further. Discount factors are normally tabulated as shown in Appendix B.

*The Yield or Rate of Return Method*

The purpose of this method is to find a rate of return for the discounting of future receipts after a given project outlay has been made. The project disbursement needs to be recovered. Normally, this will be done over a number of periods, wiih each revenue benefit making a contribution to the recovery of the outlay and servicing the interest on the outstanding amount. The greater the revenue benefits, the higher will be the interest rate at which the outstanding capital sum can be serviced. Eventually there comes a stage when all the revenue cash flows are used to repay the investment and to meet the interest charges. It is for that point of balance that we have to find the interest rate.

It should be remembered that the recovery of the investment is already included in the calculation. Therefore, no provision needs to be made for depreciation; we are simply concerned with cash flows. The subsequent disposition of these cash flows in the financial accounting context is quite a separate matter.

The general principle of the method can be shown as follows:

let $E$=the project capital expenditure

$R_i$=the project benefit in the 'i'th period ($i=1, 2, \ldots T$) measured at end of period

$T$=the expected project or equipment life

$r$=the rate of return to be established.

Allowing for the passage of time, the present value at time 0 of the future receipts will be as follows:

for $R_1$ it will be $\frac{R_1}{1+r}$

$R_3$ it will be $\frac{R_3}{(1+r)^3}$

..........................................

$R_t$ it will be $\frac{R_t}{(1+r)^t}$ etc.

The total present value (or discounted value) of these benefits will be:

$$\frac{R_1}{(1+r)} + \frac{R_2}{(1+r)^2} + \ldots \frac{R_t}{(1+r)^t} + \ldots \frac{R_T}{(1+r)^t}$$

$$= \sum_{i=1}^{i=T} \frac{R_t}{(1+r)_t}$$

For total outlay recovery this value needs to be equal to the initial investment, thus

$$\sum_{i=1}^{i=T} \frac{R_t}{(1+r)^t} = E$$

Alternatively this expression can be put in the following form:

$$\sum_{i=1}^{i=T} \frac{R_t}{(1+r)^t} - E = 0$$

The value of 'r' is the unknown in the equation and our task is to find it. When we have found the value of 'r' which solves this equation we have found the interest rate at which the project has zero net present value (NPV), *i.e.*, our immediate outlay is balanced by the future discounted receipts at that rate of interest. For all other interest rates there will not be this balance and we shall have a NPV with a value other than zero. If a particular rate is pitched too low the NPV will be positive; if our rate is too high the NPV will be negative. This property is very useful in calculating the rate of return, as we shall see in subsequent examples.

*Example 1*

Consider, initially, a new production plant with a capital cost of £ 100000, an expected working life of five years and yielding the following net cash flow (see Table 8.2).

How can we best calculate our rate of return? The first thing we note is that the net project receipts come to £150000 over the five years. We recover our investment outlay and £50000 is available for interest payments. To make a first assessment of the rate of return we calculate the project NPVs at key rates, say at 10 per cent, 20 per cent and 30 per cent. Using the discount tables in Appendix B we obtain the results shown in Table 8.3. The respective NPVs are plotted on graph paper and a net present value curve is obtained as per Figure 8.2. If the curve is laid out on a sheet of graph paper it will be noted that it will cut the zero NPV line between 16 per cent and 17 per cent. To come nearer to the actual rate of return the project NPVs are calculated for these rates. (See Table 8.4). We can now calculate the more precise rate as

$$16 + \frac{1700}{17000 + 400} = 16.8\ \%$$

Although greater accuracy is possible one should remember the approximate nature of the input data. For practical purposes the calculation need not go beyond one decimal point. The more precise discount rate can also be obtained by graphical interpolation from the two NPV figures.

Having found the rate of return for our project example we can now analyse the cash flow pattern. The cash flow for each year is divided into interest and repayment and the right column shows how the outstanding capital sum is reduced over time. The outstanding amount at the end of one year earns 16.8% interest in the next year. (See Table 8.5.) Example 1 was a relatively simple illustration of the rate of return method. If we now bring in taxation aspects we can see their discounting implications.

TABLE 8.2

| *Year* | *1* | *2* | *3* | *4* | *5* |
|---|---|---|---|---|---|
| Cash flow (£) | 40000 | 30000 | 30000 | 25000 | 25000 |

TABLE 8.3

| *Year* | *Net cash Flow £* | *At 10 %* | | *At 20 %* | | *At 30 %* | |
|---|---|---|---|---|---|---|---|
| | | *Discount factor* | *Present value* | *Discount factor* | *Present value* | *Discount factor* | *Present value* |
| 0 | (100000) | 1.000 | (100000) | 1.000 | (100000) | 1.000 | (100000) |
| 1 | 40000 | 0.909 | 36360 | 0.833 | 33320 | 0.769 | 30760 |
| 2 | 30000 | 0.826 | 24780 | 0.694 | 20820 | 0.592 | 17760 |
| 3 | 30000 | 0.751 | 22530 | 0.579 | 17370 | 0.455 | 13650 |
| 4 | 25000 | 0.683 | 17075 | 0.482 | 12050 | 0.350 | 8750 |
| 5 | 25000 | 0.621 | 15525 | 0.402 | 10050 | 0.269 | 6725 |
| Total net present value (£) | | | 16270 | | (6390) | | (22355) |

(figures in brackets are negative)

TABLE 8.4

| *Year* | *Net cash flow* (£) | *At 16%* | | *At 17%* | |
|---|---|---|---|---|---|
| | | *Discount factor* | *Present value* | *Discount factor* | *Present value* |
| 0 | (100000) | 1.000 | (100000) | 1.000 | (100000) |
| 1 | 40000 | 0.862 | 34480 | 0.855 | 34200 |
| 2 | 30000 | 0.743 | 22290 | 0.731 | 21930 |
| 3 | 30000 | 0.641 | 19230 | 0.624 | 18720 |
| 4 | 25000 | 0.552 | 13800 | 0.534 | 13350 |
| 5 | 25000 | 0.476 | 11900 | 0.456 | 11400 |
| Total net present value (£) | | | 1700 | | (400) |

TABLE 8.5

**Analysis of Cash Flow Pattern**

| *End of Year* | *Net cash flow* (£) | *Interest at 16.8%* | *Capital repayment* | *Capital outstanding* |
|---|---|---|---|---|
| 0 | (100000) | — | — | 100000 |
| 1 | 40000 | 16800 | 23200 | 76800 |
| 2 | 30000 | 12901 | 17099 | 59701 |
| 3 | 30000 | 10029 | 19971 | 39730 |
| 4 | 25000 | 6674 | 18326 | 21404 |
| 5 | 25000 | 3596 | 21404 | 0 |
| Total | | 50000 | 100000 | |

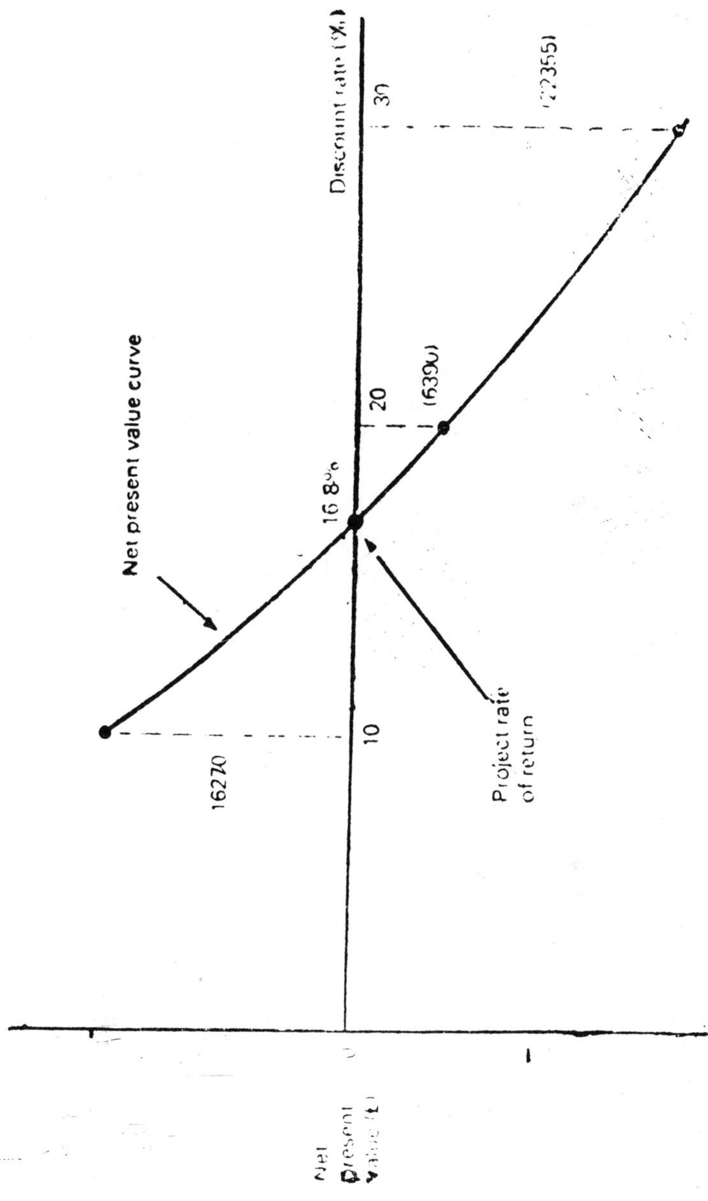


**Figure 8.2** Derivation of net present value curve

*Example 2*

For the same project assume now corporation tax at 50%, an initial plant allowance of 100% and an equipment salvage value of £5000 at the end of its working life. Tax allowances and payments normally accrue one year after the cash flow. The project computation would then look as per Table 5.6:

The relatively high rate of project return is largely the effect of the initial allowance which, by its tax saving, permits the early repayment of a substantial part of the capital expenditure. The later cash flows look correspondingly better when related to the outstanding capital sums despite the effect of corporation tax. The payment of this tax a year after the appropriate receipt is, of course, an important advantage. Should the initial allowance be less then 100% the remaining tax allowances will have to be spread over the years of accrual. The effect of the balancing charge on the plant disposal receipt should also be noted.

Example 2 can be further developed to suit particular company situations. Further cash flows, irrespective of origin or direction can readily be incorporated in the calculation.

*The Net Present Value Method*

In this alternative approach the evaluation is based on a previously specified annual rate of return—say, s%. This rate is usually based on a minimum return which the company expects to obtain from an investment before it even begins to consider it. Such a return takes into account the rate of interest which the company has to pay to attract finance, its own degree of optimism/pessimism about business prospects, a margin for project management etc. On this basis the present value of all future benefits will be

$$\sum_{i=1}^{i=T} \frac{R_t}{(1+s)^t}$$

TABLE 8.6

**Example 2—After Tax Project Rate of Return**

| Year | Capital investment | Tax saving on investment | Project income | Tax paid on project income | Net cash flow | At 17% Discount factor | At 17% Present value | At 18% Discount factor | At 18% Present value |
|---|---|---|---|---|---|---|---|---|---|
| 0 | (100000) | | | | (100000) | 1.000 | (100000) | 1.000 | (100000) |
| 1 | | 50000 | 40000 | | 90000 | 0.855 | 76950 | 0.848 | 76320 |
| 2 | | | 30000 | (20000) | 10000 | 0 731 | 7310 | 0.718 | 7180 |
| 3 | | | 30000 | (15000) | 15000 | 0.629 | 9360 | 0.609 | 9135 |
| 4 | | | 25000 | (15000) | 10000 | 0.534 | 5340 | 0 516 | 5160 |
| 5 | 5000 | | 25000 | (12500) | 17500 | 0.456 | 7980 | 0.437 | 7647 |
| 6 | | (2500) | — | (12500) | (15000) | 0.390 | (5850) | 0.370 | (5550) |
| Total | (95000) | 47500 | 150000 | 75000 | 27500 | | 1090 | | (108) |

DCF Rate of return $=17+\frac{1090}{1090+108}=17.9\%$

and the net present value (NPV) will be

$$\sum_{i=1}^{i=T} \frac{R_i}{(1+s)^i} - E$$

The higher this value the more profitable will be the investment. If the value is negative this means that the rate of return is less than the required rate set by the company. If the value is zero the project return equals the specified rate. The set rate of $s$%, of course, requires most careful consideration. The net present value technique is simple and quick in application. It has the advantage of ready comparison between a number of competitive projects, particularly if a situation of 'capital rationing' applies.

As an illustration of this method, let us assume a company specified a discount rate of 15 per cent after tax. Taking the after tax cash flow of Example 2, the tabulation would look like Table 8.7.

TABLE 8.7

| *Year* | *Net cash flow (£)* | *At 15%* *Discount factor* | *Present value* |
|---|---|---|---|
| 0 | (100000) | 1.000 | (100000) |
| 1 | 90000 | 0.870 | 78300 |
| 2 | 10000 | 0.756 | 7560 |
| 3 | 15000 | 0.658 | 9870 |
| 4 | 10000 | 0.572 | 5720 |
| 5 | 17500 | 0.497 | 8698 |
| 6 | (15000) | 0.432 | (6480) |
| Total NPV | | | £3668 |

The project NPV, at the specified company discount rate of 15 per cent, amounts to £3668.

*The Profitability Index*

Where plant projects queue for authorisation, but funds are insufficient for the total portfotio, then priority ranking becomes important. This ordering could be done on a rate of return or the NPV basis. A company may have a number of project proposals which meet the specified (or minimum) rate of return; some can be accepted, others have to be left. (Although prevalent, one hopes that this is only a short run position and that in the longer term the company can make suitable funding arrangements to take all its project opportunities.) Anyway, as funds are rationed the amounts requested become particularly important. Project scale needs to be related to project worth. However, the NPV method does not discriminate adequately between projects which vary substantially in size. For instance, project A may cost twice as much as project B but its NPV is 50 per cent higher. Superficially, it looks more attractive but its DCF return rate is, in fact, lower. This seeming dilemma can be overcome by the concept of the profitability index, PI. Using the previous notation, this can be defined by the expression

$$PI = \frac{\text{Present value of future benefits}}{\text{Project capital expenditure}} = \frac{1}{E}\left[\sum_{i=1}^{i=T} \frac{R_i}{(1+s)^i}\right]$$

Taking our example with the specified discount rate of 15 per cent, our profitability index would be 103668/100000= 1.03668. Alternatively, one can use the net present value contribution (NPVC) per £ of invested funds. We would then have

$$NPVC = \frac{\text{Project NPV}}{\text{Project capital expenditure}} = \frac{1}{E}\left[\sum_{i=1}^{i=T} \frac{R_i}{(1+s)^i} - E\right] = PI - 1$$

The NPVC for our previous example will be 0.03668, *i.e.* every £ invested would not only earn the required interest at 15 per cent but would also produce an equivalent gain of 3.668 pence.

Bromwich[1], in his study of capital budgeting, illustrates the use of profitability indices in the fund rationing situation.

### *Applying the DCF Technique*

Discounted cash flow is not only a convenient tool for plant investment appraisal; it can also be applied to many related problems, particularly in the project preparation stage. There are also variants of the technique, such as the cash flow ratio chart approach developed by Tack[2] for the economic appraisal of numerically controlled machine tools. Kingshott[3] provides a good summary of more specialised techniques, some of which take into account the re-investment opportunities for the rapid capital components during the project life. The application of such techniques, however, transcends the production context and belongs more to the realm of financial management. In this section we shall confine ourselves to some special aspects and applications of the method.

*The long construction project.* So far we have assumed for the purpose of appraisal that capital expenditure was instantaneous at the beginning of the project period. Bearing in mind the time scale of a substantial project, this assumption is somewhat artificial. The cash outflow often approximates an S curve and with such projects as a new oil refinery or power station the planned time scale of construction will be several years. Late deliveries postpone payments and the cash position can be further affected by project slippage.

Essentially, there are two approaches to this type of proposition. Consider a plant which will take two years to construct and will earn an income for the following eight years. In the first approach everything will be discounted to year 0, the beginning of the project, Subsequent capital expenditures will be discounted just like any other cash flow. The first project benefit will be discounted on a year three instead of a year one basis and later receipts, being in the more distant future, will have corresponding lower present values.

The alternative is to take the project completion date after which the plant revenues are expected to accrue. The project benefits for calendar years three to ten will now be related to an end of year two or beginning of year three base line and then discounted as if they were project years one to eight. On the other hand, all capital expenditures incurred before the end of the year two base line will be *compounded*, not discounted. It is just as if the value of 'i' in our general formula had a minus sign. The discounting base line could be drawn anywhere within a project life; what matters is that the time relationship between capital expenditures and project benefits is properly evaluated.

*The discounting time interval.* The reader will have noted the convention of the year-end computation of cash flows. This is mainly a matter of convenience and most discount tables are based on this practice. It reflects the end of year accounting approach which verifies cash flow expectations. Some writers prefer mid-year discounting as being more realistic with ongoing operations. Any period could be used for discounting. All it means is that the term 'i' is no longer an integer (whole number). Discount factors can be interpolated from annual tables or worked out from first principles with a pocket calculator.

A more sophisticated approach is continuous discounting. Some companies find it convenient to treat their project benefits on an accruals basis, particularly where monthly operating statements are used for control and decision purposes. A monthly series of project benefits approximates a continuous flow and in such cases continuous discounting techniques are suitable. The summation of discrete benefits, annual lumps of cash, is replaced by the integration of a continuous revenue stream. The notation is that of the calculus of exponential series. The main purpose of this technique is to obtain greater accuracy when large outlays and/or high interest rates are involved. A number of specialist techniques based on this concept of continuous discounting have been well summarised by Masse.[4]

*Incremental analysis.* DCF analysis can form part of an appraisal at any stage of the project preparation process. For instance, it can help in working out the optimum plant size. In some processes there are great economies of scale with the construction of large plants, but we may have to face under-utilisation of capacity. It is worth it? Incremental analysis can provide a quick answer.

Consider Example No. 1. If we now had an alternative production unit with 20% extra capacity and costing £120000, would this be worthwhile if the net cash flow is lifted by £5000 per annum for the five years? In its simplest form the choice could be represented as in Table 8.8.

TABLE 8.8

| *Year* | *First unit cash flow* (£) | *Alternative plant cash flow* (£) | *Incremental values* (£) |
|---|---|---|---|
| 0 | (100000) | (120000) | (20000) |
| 1 | 40000 | 45000 | 5000 |
| 2 | 30000 | 35000 | 5000 |
| 3 | 30000 | 35000 | 5000 |
| 4 | 25000 | 30000 | 5000 |
| 5 | 25000 | 30000 | 5000 |
| DCF rate | 16.8% | | 7.9% |

We note that the extra investment of £20000 provides a return of 7.9 per cent. Clearly this is not an impressive yield and suggests that the first unit should be chosen.

Incremental analysis has many applications in project evaluation where variants to a basic proposal are considered, such as with the choice of a process route, replacement problems or the lease/buy decision.

### *The Problem of Inflation*

Inflation accounting is a contentious business. There is no agreed view as to how inflation should be allowed for in project appraisal. The experience of the last ten years in most countries has been that inflation is a significant, if not serious, factor in the health of a national economy. Its unpredictability is awkward for business calculations but it will not go away just because it is inconvenient. Various cash flow constituents can have different inflation rates; for example, labour costs could rise faster than raw material prices. There are valuation problems and tax complications. What can be done? A number of solutions are offered.

1. One school of thought advocates that project appraisal should ignore inflation. With a long time scale, forecasts are likely to be wrong anyway. The response should be at the operating management level which can adjust prices, plant values and depreciation rates as and when appropriate.

2. An alternative is to index all revenue and cost elements at their expected inflation rates before carrying out the evaluation. With the passage of time the original capital expenditure will look small in current monetary terms and the return on the investment could look disproportionately and misleadingly high.

3. The next approach is to adjust asset values to correspond to current replacement costs. This is not an easy task when there is a great range of specialist

equipment supplied in a narrow market and possibly affected by technical change. Nevertheless, in conjunction with method 2, this obviates some of the overstatement of returns related to historical capital costs.

4. Another alternative is to express all future cash flows in terms of the monetary values as at the evaluation or the capital expenditure stage. Future sales, costs, returns, etc., would all be correspondingly diminished. This might make the prospect more sobering for the evaluators.

5. Finally, a simple device would be to allow for the inflation rate in the minimum acceptable rate of return. For instance, if we take our previous example of a company cut-off rate of 15 per cent and inflation is at 8 per cent, a crude adjustment would be to make the new required rate 23 per cent. This would still, however, underestimate the allowance for inflation. Consider an investment of £100 to be repaid at the end of one year. To maintain the purchasing power of this investment we need to have £108 at the end of the period. Again, the interest payment at the end of the year needs to be maintained in real terms, so this will also have to be multiplied by 1.08. Generally, the adjusted rate of return 'R' with a required real term interest rate 'r' and inflation at 'i' per cent will be given by the relationship.

$$R = r + i \ (1 + \frac{r}{100}).$$

here $$R = 15 + 8 \ (1 + \frac{15}{100}) \ = 24.2 \text{ per cent}$$

This general relationship for a given year can be extended over longer periods with (or without) varying inflation rates for different years, The calculation can be further refined by using 'second-order' techniques, such as sensitivity analysis. These will be developed in Chapter 6.

Which of the various solutions to adopt may be a matter of business judgement. One thing is certain; to do nothing about inflation is equivalent to an economic death-warrant. Solutions are not always easy; for instance, a price uplift to maintain revenue in real terms can lead to marketing problems if competitors are underpricing their products because of their unadjusted accounting basis. The first thing a company should endeavour to do is to maintain the real value of its assets and revenues. Its management accounting system, the framework for operational decisions, should use figures which are telling in this respect. Consistency in use comes next, whatever the adopted basis for evaluation and accounting. For example, there must be no manipulation of forecast inflation rates to make a doubtful proposition passable.

**Reminder**

The appraisal of projects is a quantitative task. The required techniques are well written up in text books and can be readily applied. In doing our calculations, with or without computer, and getting our yields, we might be tempted into smugness and forget how dependent our figures are on the assumptions and expectations of others. A critical approach to every input figure needs to be maintained. Appraisal without audit is mere arithmetic.

**Check List: Project Evaluation**

*General*

1. Is the project within established policies and objectives?
2. Is the project technically and operationally sound?
3. Who makes the detailed evaluation?
4. Who checks this evaluation?

*Specific Project Aspects*

1. Who is the basis of project benefit? Cost reduction? Extra contribution from expansion?
2. Have you obtained all *incremental benefits and costs* due to the project?
3. On what basis and assumptions have these been established?
4. Have the specialists responsible for such computations confirmed or endorsed them in writing?
5. What project alternatives have been examined? Different plant sizes, location or processes?
6. What is the horizon, in years, for project calculations?
7. Have all tax allowances and special grants been taken into account?
8. Has the latest corporation tax rate been used in the evaluation of generated project benefits?
9. What provisions have been made for

   (a) contingencies,

   (b) escalation of project costs,

   (c) inflation effects on future operations,

   (d) redundancy payments where labour is reduced?
10. What is the required discount rate, net present value, rate of return or payback period? How does the proposal relate to these?
11. What are the main risks of the proposition? Establish the most pessimistic, likely and optimistic combination of circumstances and project outcomes.
12. Have you carried out a sensitivity analysis on the key project parameters?

13. Is the project part of a chain of development? If so, what are the subsequent decisions that need to be taken?

14. What is the project cash flow pattern? How does it look in a graphical form?

15. What happens if you do not proceed with the project? Are there meaningful alternatives?

## REFERENCES

1. Bromwich, M., *The Economics of Capital Budgeting*, Penguin Books (Harmondsworth, Middlesex, 1976).
2. Tack, A., 'Economic Appraisal,' see Leslie, W.H.P., (Ed.) *Numerical control users' handbook*. Chapter 4, McGraw-Hill (London, 1970).
3. Kingshott, A.L., *Investment Appraisal*, Ford Business Library (Brentwood, Essex, 1967).
4. Masse, P., *Optimal Investment Decisions*, Prentice-Hall (Englewood Cliffs, N.J., 1962).

## FURTHER RECOMMENDED READING

1. Merrett, A.J., & Sykes, A., *The Finance and Analysis of Capital Projects*, Longmans, (London 1963).
2. Murdick, R.G., and Deming, D.D., *The Management of Capital Expenditures*, McGraw-Hill, (New York, 1968).
3. Wright, R.W., *Investment Decisions in Industry*, Chapman Hall, (London, 1964).
4. Dean, J., *Capital Budgeting*, Columbia University Press, (New York, 1962).

# 9

# PHYSICAL AND FINANCIAL MONITORING OF PROJECTS

V. RANGANATHAN*

With increasing investments in the Public Sector Projects, timely completion of these project has become a crucial factor in the very profitabifity of these projects. But the past experience in this regard is far from reassuring. To cite an extreme example, the Madras Atomic Power Project phase I was originally expected to "go critical" in December 1974. water it was revised to March 1977. Till date the project is not yet commissioned and now the project authorities do not even indicate the re-revised target date for commissioning. There are other examples which are less severs in character. Major delays like these have three important implications:

1. Large cost over-runs.
2. Large social opportunity costs arising out of the product not being available, and
3. In the case of inter-dependent projects, the delay of one project leads to the delay of other projects dependent on its.

*Mr. Ranganathan is Assistant Professor at I.I.M. Bangalore.

For enabling better management of projects, a properly designed Project Monitoring System is a *sine-qua-non.* It should be capable of performing the following functions:

1. Cost Control
2. Budgetary request/sanction
3. Progress reporting and highlighting hold-ups
4. Cash Flow
5. External Agency Reporting.

In the present article an attempt has been made to design such a Project Monitoring System, based on the experience the author gained at the National Thermal Power Corporation. The system is especially suitable for Public Sector Projects, which normally have long gestation periods. The System is described below:

**Objectives**

1. To get up-to-date information on equipment and eraction costs, sub-system-wise.
2. To get information on cost over-run, due to:
   (a) increase in material prices and wages
   (b) delay-escalation for the delay period and/or cost of crashing certain activities to keep to the schedule.
   (c) under-estimation in the Detailed Project report.
3. To enable proper and uniform presentation of Budget request.
4. To substantiate the Budget request in terms of physical programme. For the sanctioning authority, to evaluate the Budget request.

5. To provide information to mangement on past performance—comparison of actual physical and financial progress with budgeted figures.

6. To enable preparation of projected cash flows.

7. To evolve estimation of man days for various activities of each sub-system.

8. To allocate indirect, expenditures to various subsystems to build up sub-system-wise total expenditures and ultimately sub-system-wise total costs (by adding the indirect component to the direct).

9. To compare actual indirect expenditures with the establishment charges in Detailed Project Report.

10. To create a Data Bank to help compute more accurate project cost estimates in future. Greater accuracy will result from (a) detailing, instead of making lumpsum estimates (b) better apprecation of the range of escalation for each sub-system instead of lumpsum celling.

**Methodology**

Objectives 1 and 2 are achieved through Form 1. The form will present data on:

1. D.P.R. estimate
2. Original contract value and
3. Cost over-run

The cost over-run is sub-divided into: (a) escalation (without any delay) (b) escalation due to delay, and (c) extra costs of crashing to keep to the schedule, in case of delays.

It is possible to separately document each of these reasons since actual expenditure figures will be available.

In determining the current value of the contract, cost over-run (a) will apply to the full contract; cost-over-run (b) will apply to the extent of actual delay till the date of filling up the form, and cost over-run (c) will apply depending on the judgement about which activities will be crashed and their extra cost evaluated as on the day of filling up the form.

Variance percentages are calculated as the variations of contract value over DPR (col. 17) and actual over contract value (cols. 18 and 19). The latter is further split into increase due to escalations (without delay) and due to delays. Col. 17 can be looked upon either as an index of efficiency of the contracts department, or as a measure of underestimation of DPR. Column 18 reflects contributions due to uncontrollable factors like global inflation. Col. 19 reflects the contribution of delays to cost over-run.

Objectives 3, 4, 5 and 6 are sought to be achieved by Form 2. Here an attempt is made to link up the physical programme according to PERT network with the Budget request. The various components of the physical programme are converted into a single physical progress index (PPI) which is a constant fraction of the total programme connected with the related contract, and the Budget request is arrived at by multiplying the total contract value by this fraction (index of physical progress). The development of this index is described below.

*Development of the Index.* For this purpose, all activities are broadly divided into two types:

1. those relating to indirect costs, and
2. those relating to direct costs,

Activities relating to indirect costs do not involve payment to contractor. These are broadly:

1. Design and engineering
2. Preparation of specification

3. Tender issue

4. Tender receipt

5. Tender evaluation

6. Placement of letter of indent

7. Release of construction/manufacturing/erection drawing.

The PPI does not include the above activities, since these activities do not result in direct costs, and are taken into account in formulating the manpower budget and salaries budget.

Activities involving direct costs are:

1. Equipment ordering,

2. Manufacture and supply, and

3. Erection.

One index for activities 1 and 2 is developed, and the index for activity 3 is developed separately, though along the same lines.

Schedule of payments have to be developed for each contract earmarking a certain percentage of payment for each activity. Some of the activies are further divided in terms of materials despatched/received or percentage of erection completed within such activities. The PPI is measured along the same scale as the payment schedule. An example is given below:

Supposing that the payment schedule of a Boiler as per the original tender is as follows;

| *Activity* | *Index of progress (percentage of payment)* |
|---|---|
| Equipment ordering | 20 per cent |
| Material despatch | 55 per cent |
| Material receipt | 15 per cent |
| End of warranty | 10 per cent |
| Total | 100 per cent |

Then if the material despatch and material receipt are spread over a long period for actual payment purposes it is necessary to further subdivide the figures 55 and 17 on the basis of a chosen numeraire for each item of supply or erection *e.g.* tonnes, cubic metres, numbers etc.

Let the fraction of total material despatch $=x$

And fraction of total material received $=y$

The PPI$=.20+.55x+.15y$, and the actual payment will have to be made on the basis of this index.

In the case of cumulative past performance x and y will represent cumulative fractions and in the case or bugeted performance they will present budget fractions.

It is to be noted that the figures 55 and 15 presenting percentage payments are noting but the composite rates, *i.e.*, rates for the entre activity. Thus, any two activities having different units of measurement are made commensurable by weighing them by their money values or composite rates. This procedure is repeated for finding the overall progress of various contracts be weighing progress indices of individual contracts by the monetary fraction (based on original estimates).

In most activities the actual physical progress and the financial progress may not match because of the existence of:

1. Advance payments, which made before and physical progress is achieved, and
2. Payments which are made at the end of warranty period *i.e.*, after considerable time after 100 per cent physical progress is made. The situation is depicted below.

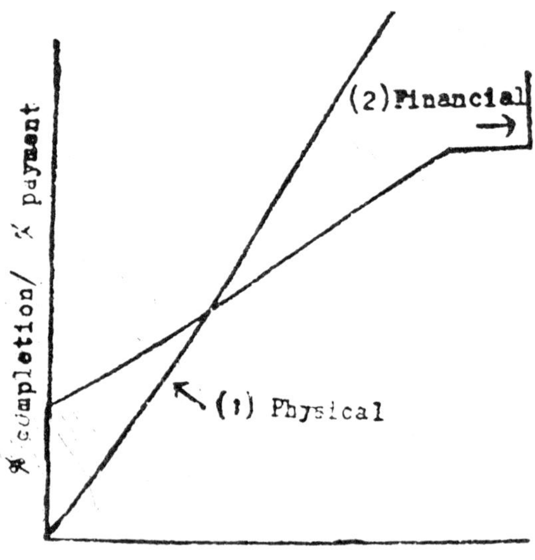


Figure 9.1

| *Year* | *0* | *1* | *2* | *3* | *4* | *5* |
|---|---|---|---|---|---|---|
| Payment | | (50-10) | (50-10) | (50-10) | (50-10) | (50-10) |
| Schedule | 50 | =40 | =40 | =40 | =40 | =40 |
| PPI | 20 | 36 | 52 | 68 | 84 | 100 |

**Figure 9.2**

For better monetary control and easier communication while reporting, it is desirable to achieve a one-to-one correspondence between physical and financial progress. For this purpose, P.P.I. itself is based on the payment schedule. This being so, it under lines the necessity of matching as closely as possible, the payments in each contract to the actual work/material input by the contractor, so that the two lines in the above grap are brought as close to each other as possible.

In civil contracts, unlike in mechanical and electrical equipment contracts the initial advance amount is adjusted during that progress of work. The index must reflect this aspect. For example, suppose the value of contract is Rs. 250 and the contract runs for 5 periods with equal effort. Let advance amount paid initially be Rs. 50, which is adjusted as Rs. 10 instalment. (see Figure 9.2).

The last item in Form 2 (columns 17 to 20) gives the quarterly phasing of expenditures worked out in an analogous manner. Since the quarterly budget requests will be derived from the physical indices and since the sum for the 4 quarters has to march the request for the year, corresponding quarter-wise indices are not asked for.

Objective 7 is to evolve estimation of man days for various activities of each subsystem. The ultimate aim is to optimise manpower by striking a balance between project delays and over-staffing. This is one of the important areas where scope for minimising cost over-run exists in a large measure. At present, for several new projects, we do not have man-hour standards for various activities and have only a rough estimate of establishment charges. Even here no 'systematic method has been attempted to arrive at a reference estimate of man-power input for the various activities constituting the indirect costs. This is sought to be achieved by the introduction of a job time booking card (Form 3) which will be filled by all the employees concerned, other than those belonging to training. personnel, accounts and corporate planning. While the man-power budget for the training departmenr will be a derived budget based on requests from other departments, the manpower budget for finance and personnel departments, will be based on a constant proportion to the total staff strength in the other departments, since they are related in a may to the number of employees to be served. As regards Corporate Planning, the management can directly derive the manpower without recourse to norms.

It is envisaged that continuous operation of the job-time booking card system will ultimately result in the evolution of man-hour strandards for various activities, which can then be used as reference yardsticks for future projects, and in some cases for the later stages of the current project itself.

Objectives 8 and 9 *i.e.*, allocation of indirect expenditures to sub-systems to get their total costs, and to compare the actual indirect costs with the establishment charges (contained in the DPR)—are easily actievable once the job-time-booking card system is implemented. Allocational bases will be derived from the above system and the indirect expenditures/costs will be allocated to each contract if possible, or to the sub-system.

Form 4 details how the sub-system-wise total costs are arrived at by combining the direct costs, indirect costs and interest, and also gives a comparison between the actual indirect costs allocated and the per cent of establishment charges, as contained in the DPR. (For aligning the terminology with that of the accounting system, the indirect expenditures will be referred to as 'incidental expenditure during construction).

Objective 10 is to create a Data Bank to help generate more accurate cost estimates. This Data Bank will also contain man-hour standards for various activities. The Data Bank will also store other important data, like various rate schedules, employee statistics, and other data relating to the preparation of Project Feasibility Report.

The above forms are designed with a view to helping the Budget preparation/sanction, and to monitor physical and financial progress. It is also necessary to institute devices which may help to ensure that the projects do run on schedule. Form 5 is designed for such a purpose. It helps to ensure that each activity starts on time, by making the preparatory work beforehand. It also serves as a feedback mechanism to incorporate on-line revisions on project completion dates. At a stage when the Master PERT network is computerised, the revised dates for each activity from individual departments will determine the new critical path from time to time, and hence update the project's overall slippage.

The form also builds into it exception monitoring—columns (10) and (11) report expected slippages and the reasons thereof, and invite the attention of the management for taking higher level remedial actions. Incidentally for Power Projects, this ties in with the reporting requirement of the Central Electricity Authority.[1]

**Assumptions and Pre-requisites**

1. A Master network (PERT) is prepared with the concurrence of the departments concerned as regards the realism of the end dates given to them for working within.

2. The concerned departments will do detailed planning and submit detailed network (blowing up the end points given to them) along with the budget request. In the case of time constraint for such an exercise, the level of detailing may be broad initially and further fine tuning taken up later on.

3. Since the physical progress index is based on the schedule of payments, it is assumed that in each contract every endeavour is made to pay the contractor an amount commensurate with his work/material input. This is done to some extent by synchronising the contractor's PERT with the master network and accordingly working out the payment schedule.

4. The various rate schedules are available.

**Specific Exclusions Which the Present Paper Does Not Cover**

1. Effect of the delay of several individual activities upon the delay of project—change of critical paths—opportunity costs of delay.

2. Details of building up the data bank.

3. Man-hour control: At present only activity-wise man-hour input information is sought. The next step will be the setting up of man-hour standards by deleting the idex hours from total hours spent on activities. The third step will be the control of future activities with reference to these man-hour standards.

4. The process of Budgetary control is to naturally link with Performance Appraisal, this in turn linking with a Reward/Punishment system. This can be done once the standard cost of each Budget centre is arrived at, by relating the actual cost with standard cost. (*i.e.*, each budget centre is an investment centre). But now, even though we have identified the budget centres as identical with each sub-system, we have not yet established a relationship between Responsibility centres and Budget centres. This is because, the Organization structure and the responsibilities of each department over the portion of the Master PERT network will have to be established for each organization separately.

5. An exercise for detailed physical progress monitoring is to be undertaken (that is, who will do what and feed information to whom) concurently.

6. Financial powers related to Budgetary levels are to specified separately in the Detailed Delegation of Powers.

1. Interested readers may refer to Forms $T_1$, $T_2$ and $T_3$ of the CEA's reporting requirements.

**Form 1**

## PROJECT COSTS AND OVER-RUNS

### Contracts: Mechanical Equipment

(a) Subsystems completed (b) Subsystems in process

| Subsystem Contract No. and Date | D.P R. Estimate | | | Original contract value | | |
|---|---|---|---|---|---|---|
| | Equipment | Erection | Total | Equipment | Erection | Total |
| 1 | 2 | 3 | 4 | 5 | 6 | 7 |

Form 1 (*Continued*)
For Quarter No. I/II/III/IV

Date:

Figures in Rs. '000

| Increase due to mtaerial prices and wages | | | Increase due to delay | | | Current contract value | | | Variance percentages | | |
|---|---|---|---|---|---|---|---|---|---|---|---|
| Equipment | Erection | Total | Equipment | Erection | Total | Equipment | Erection | Total | 1 $\frac{(7)\quad(4)}{(4)}$ | 2 $\frac{(10)}{(7)}$ | 3 $\frac{(13)}{(7)}$ |
| 8 | 9 | 10 | 11 | 12 | 13 | 14 | 15 | 16 | 17 | 18 | 19 |

*Note*: 1. In cases where varianee exceeds Rs. 5 lakhs or 10 per cent of the DPR estimate (wherever is less). Please explain such variations.

2. Form to be filled by Site Accounts and submitted to Corporate Finance through conccrned Department Head and Site G.M.

**Form 2**

## BUDGET REQUEST/SANCTION

**Contracts: Mechanical Equipment**

(a) Subsystems in progress (b) Subsystems to be taken up

| Subsystem Contract No. and Date | Current value of contract | | | Equipment Index of progress | | | Expenditure | | |
|---|---|---|---|---|---|---|---|---|---|
| | Equipment | Erection | Total | Cumulative Budget | Past Actual | Present Budget | Cumulative Budget | Past Actual | Present Budget |
| 1 | 2 | 3 | 4 | 5 | 6 | 7 | 8 | 9 | 10 |

Form 2 (*Continued*)

Figures Rs. '000

| Erection Total Index of Progress | | | Expenditure | | | Phasing of Expenditure | | | |
|---|---|---|---|---|---|---|---|---|---|
| Cumulative Budget | Past Actual | Present Budget | Cumulative Budget | Past Actual | Present Budget | I Qr | II Qr | II Qr | IV Qr |
| 11 | 12 | 13 | 14 | 15 | 16 | 17 | 18 | 19 | 20 |

*Note*: Index of progress for each contract will be worked out by the initiating Departments in advance of all such contracts and a separate document is to be made available to Corporate Planning and Corporate Finance Departments.

**Form 3**

## JOB TIME BOOKING CARD

Employee No....... ......                                        Dept. No.................

| Activity (i, j) | Time taken (Days) | | Reason for Delay (if any) |
|---|---|---|---|
| | Budget | Actual | |
| 1 | 2 | 3 | 4 |
| | | | |

**Form 4**

## EXPENDITURE STATUS

### Contracts: Equipment

(a) Subsystems completed (b) Subsystems in process (c) Subsystems to be taken up

| Sub-system Contract No. and Date | Actual expenditure on equipment and erection upto the end of previous year | | | Budgeted expenditure on equipment and erection for the year | | | Incidential expenditure during construction | | Interest allocated | | Progressive expenditure | | | IECD as a % of equipment and errection | % of estt. charges as DPR |
|---|---|---|---|---|---|---|---|---|---|---|---|---|---|---|---|
| | Eqpt. | Erection charges | Total | Eqpt. | Erection charges | Total | Comulative actual | Budgeted | Comulative actual | Budgeted | Comulative actual 4+8+10 | Budgeted 7+9 +11 | Total 12+13 | Expenditure $\frac{8+10 \times 100}{4}$ | |
| 1 | 2 | 3 | 4 | 5 | 6 | 7 | 8 | 9 | 10 | 11 | 12 | 13 | 14 | 15 | 16 |

**Form 5**

## PROJECT i-j SCHEDULE

| Sl. No. | Sub system and Contract No. | Activity Node No. i | Activity Node No. j | Activity Description | Scheduled Week Start | Duration of Activity | Scheduled Completion Week | Expected Completion Week | Expected Slippage if any (9)—(8) | Reason |
|---|---|---|---|---|---|---|---|---|---|---|
| 1 | 2 | 3 | 4 | 5 | 6 | 7 | 8 | 9 | 10 | 11 |
| | | | | | | | | | | |

*Note*: 1. Projects activity node No. I should be listed in the chronological order of the week of starting.

# 10

# THE PROJECT OUTCOME EVALUATION

We now come to the final stages of the plant investment process. The project funds have been spent; results are now expected. Figure 12.1 shows the remaining activities: those concerned with the project outcome and its evaluation.

## Plant Commissioning

The new buildings are ready, the equipment is in position, all connections and circuits have been completed. Operating personnel are standing by to begin the plant commissioning task. It is the optimist, perhaps the layman, who would describe this activity as 'switching on.' Plant commissioning is often a complex business. Its first objective is to establish whether the installed plant works; whether it is capable of achieving the pysical tasks that are expected from it. The second objective is to confirm whether the plant can work to design and operational specifications. That is a major step in the economic realisation of the project intent.

The commissioning task can have many components. With process plants, such as in the food or drug industries, it can mean thorough washing out and sterilisation. The equipment might have to be purged with inert gases, charged with catalysts

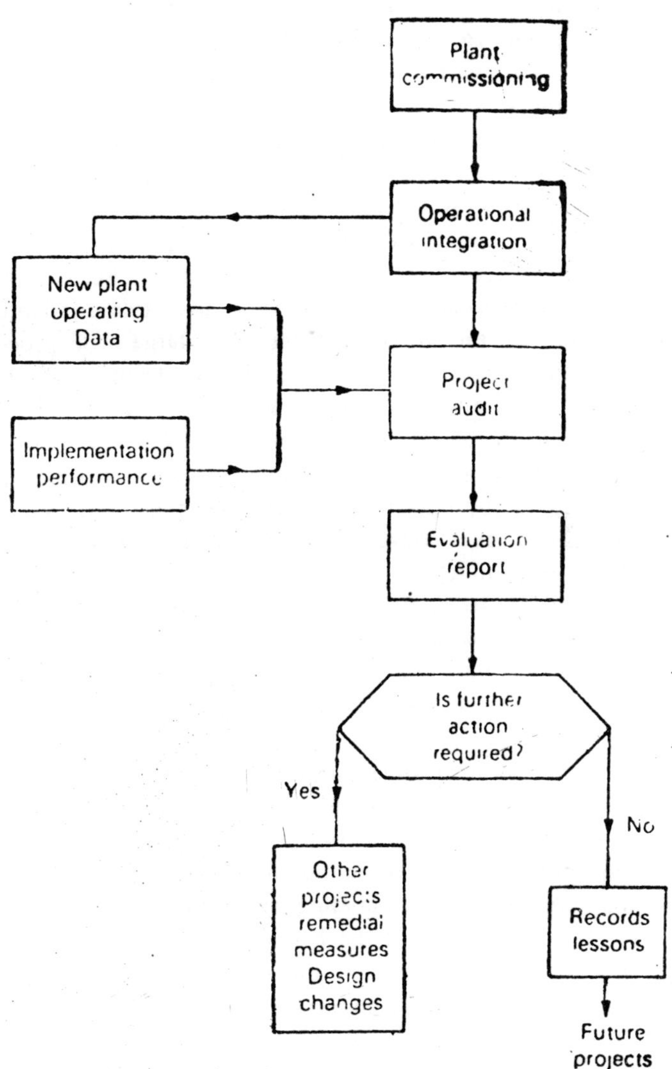


**Figure 10.1** The project outcome evaluation process

or chemicals. Services, such as steam or compressed air, may have to be fed to the plant, all moving parts need to be lubricated, all control circuits and warning devices set. Operators and supervisors are often new to the type of plant. A vital stage of ther training and familiarisation occurs when the detailed plant behaviour is not yet really known. Commissioning assistance may be given by plant suppliers as part of their contract. In other cases licensors may furnish specialists as part of a know-how agreement. Such staff is invaluable but expensive and often only available for limited periods. One of the great problems with large-scale process plants is the operational blending of the various sub-units. Each might operate without too much difficulty as a separate unit, but overall balance and stability is not easily achieved. To all this must be added the risks due to, and at times the damage caused by, the unexpected, the oversights, errors, carelessness and other relevant ingredients of human imperfection. Discrete production units, such as machine tools, are relatively simple to commission, but the problems compound with complex, automated equipment. If operating conditions are severe or the materials processed are dangerous then plant commissioning can be quite hazardous.

This tells in terms of time and money. Commissioning may take weeks, even months. Some plants never properly leave the commissioning stage because they fail to achieve the set operating specification. Despite modifications the plant remains 'de-rated'. During the commissing stage the plant is in the nursery. Often it draws on the best operating and supervisory staff, in a crisis management too might stay and even work on the shop floor! Output may be erratic but costs will be consistently heavy. Commissioning expenses and delays often have an adverse effect on the first year of operation. A good project proposal makes provision for such a contingency, but accurate forecasts may be difficult to make.

Plant commissioning experiences furnish much of the information relevant to project outcome evaluation. They are one of the major indicators of project success or failure. In the latter case further capital expenditure might rectify the troubles experienced, but in overall project terms the original promise or proposition has then been qualified.

**Operational Integration**

This consists of the transformation of the commissioned plant into an ordinary production unit. Where the commissioning process has not been afflicted by too many 'teething troubles' operational integration may follow quickly and the two stages may blend into each other. The extra attention and support provided for plant commissioning is withdrawn in stages as more becomes known about plant performance and reliability. This is particularly so where a plant shows 'burn-in' characteristics, *i.e.*, where a number of initial failures are expected before the equipment settles down to a steady operating condition. The plant acquires the status of an ordinary ordinary production unit—it is weaned, so to speak—when special considerations need no longer be given to the various aspects of its operations. Appropriate production standards have been established and can be maintained; operating personnel are familiar with experienced in the process.

Successful plant commissioning is no guarantee, of course, of effective operational integration. Some technical problems, such as corrosion, may not be apparent during the start-up phase. Envisaged work routines are not always confirmed in practice. Some retraining or work rearrangement may be necessary. The latter can give rise to manning disputes and other industrial relations problems. The stoppages due to these can easily outstrip the losses due to breakdowns. There can be much variation in the time scale of operational integrations. Where it has led to, or has been used for, 'political embroilment,' the time scale may extend to years.

When the operational integration of the new plant has been completed or all efforts have been made towards its attainment, then the last stage of the investment process has been reached. This last stage is often known as the *project audit.* It is, in essence, a total review of the project, a compariosn, in all respects, of performance with promise. This chapter is mainly concerned with this last phase—the evaluation of the project outcome.

**Project Outcome Evaluation**

When we refer to the project outcome we consider all the incremental changes that can be ascribed in a total situation to the advent and completion of a particular project. This includes the plant operation of the thereby created.

Such a wide interpretation of the term 'project outcome' provides two opportunities for further exploration:

1. It includes the assessment of both quantitative and non-quantitative changes.
2. It enables as broad a comparison as possible to be made between project promise and project outcome.

Of course, the incremental changes can be numerous; for instance, in just one functional area, say manufacture, we can have changes in production rates, productivity, labour utilisation, etc For the convenience of analysis such changes can be aggregated under the following main headings:

1. Economic changes. These are normally quantified in financial terms.
2. Technical changes. These are seen in terms of the interpretation given in Table 10.2.
3. Operational changes. These can be viewed as changes in the pattern of work organisation and the manning required for the production task.
4. Behavioural changes. We are concerned here with individual and working group relationships.

### *Problems of Outcome Evaluation*

Not much has been written about the practice of project audits. We are in a difficult and somewhat sensitive area here. Systematic outcome evaluation requires a comprehensive project follow-up procedure. The main obstacles affecting the development of such a follow-up system can be summarised as follows:

1. The difficulty of isolating the purely incremental project changes from other developments in a dynamic situation.
2. Problems of result apportionment in a multi-activity setting, particularly in a conflict situation.
3. The nature of subjective judgement involved in the consideration of intangible benefit claims.
4. The implicit nature of many assumptions which underlie benefit computation.

Despite these difficulties, a certain amount of project audit can be seen in practice, particularly where the unit can be readily isolated as a profit or cost centre. Attention is also given to those project aspects which are more readily observed and measured, typically the following:

1. the project time schedule.
2. project capital cost data
3. plant performance data
4. plant manning data
5. product sales forecasts
6. product quality standards.

The nature of the plant commissioning process is often such that attention will be given to details of plant performance, particularly if these have contractual implications, such as the retention of monies. Again if a particular project aspect shows a decisive change for the worse, then management is usually forced into a special investigation. However, apart from such cases there is little incentive for detailed investigation at the operational level if the plant satisfies the operating specifications

*The Concept of Investment Control*

The most significant attempt to put project evaluation on a systematic footing has been made by Luder. In his view investment control has two components. The first is essentially a series of project audits which evaluate the performance of a production unit over a period of years, if necessary.

His basic concept was expressed by the following relationships:

$$A = E_w - E_t = A(D, S, M)$$

where $A$ = project outcome variance

$E_w$ = budgeted project outcome

$E_t$ = actual project outcome

Also A is a function of:

D = degree of completeness of the project data

S = accuracy limits of the data

M = the degree of data manipulation

(Manipulation is not meant to derogatory here. It refers to the transcription of data originally intended for other purposes.) These factors, in turn, are dependent on the levels of decision preparation and project control. It is difficult to measure factors such as D or M. The concept does not provide a technique but a general way of looking at projects which is helpful for comparisons.

## An Approach to Project Outcome Evaluation

There are two basic project categories where the scope and worth of project evaluation seem to be in question. One is the very simple project where the task looks hardly worthwhile, particularly if the claimed benefits are obvious to all. The other is the project in a complex, fast-changing setting where the prospect of meaningful evaluation looks too daunting. Even if these categories were accepted as unrewarding, many important projects could still be evaluated to advantage.

### *The Case for the Project Audit*

What justifies the task of project audit ? Like all instruments of review and control it must justify itself in cost/benefit terms. It is not a matter of mere curiosity nor should it be the vehicle for a witch-hunt. It is done for the information and lessons which it yields and makes available as an ingredient of future managerial decision-taking. An audit can confirm the need for corrective action. It provides guidelines for the assessment of similar, subsequent project submissions. The feedback can be used for future project preparation work, particularly where this is done away from the plant location. It has a training dimension and a tinge of discipline.

With many companies there is a large gap between the overall return on capital employed and the returns claimed for plant projects. One would have thought that a project which shows a return of only 5 per cent or 6 per cent is not economically justifiable. Yet when we look at capital employed which is largely an aggregate of past invesment projects, including both fixed assets and working capital, then we often find such returns in practice. No duobt, there are many reasons, and reasons, and scapegoats, for the difference between company and project rates of return. The ultimate yield of a project audit can be seen in the reduction of this gap.

Where a company has many projects it will be useful to specify a project value above which, in the absence of good cause, an audit shall be carried out. Below this is asampling approach can be used. Understandably, companies are often reluctant about taking on more staff for such review duties. However, staffing aspects are less crucial where established project audit procedure reduces the task content. Where a large firm already has an internal audit section, project audit can be part of its remit. Alternatively, estimating sections and management accounting departments may already be involved in project preparation and implementation monitoring. They have much of the needed background. The project audit task can also be made parts of a management development programme, where future senior staff learn more about the art of dissecting complex situations.

*The Timing of the Project Audit*

The intent of the project audit is to get a fair and proper view of how a plant project turned out. It needs to be done after the operational integration when, so to speak, a 'steady state' has been reached. Before then, one could still get performance fluctuations as the plant is in the process of settling down. If it is left too long the accretions of subsequent decisions and changes need to be isolated. This becomes more difficult with time.

*The Substance of the Project Audit*

The task of the project audit is to establish the project costs and returns and to compare these with the forecasts on which the project was authorised. This will then give the variance on the project return. By the time of the audit the project accounts should give a good picture of the capital expenditure incurred and the investigation could concentrate on the varification of project benefits.

Much of this will be a repetition of the original benefit computation but with actual, not expected, data. Have all the stated changes in costs actually taken place and to the amounts

TABLE 10.1a

**Sample Project Audit Data**

| *Item* | *Year 1 forecast* (£) | *Year 1 actual* (£) | *Variance* (£) |
|---|---|---|---|
| Tooling | 12000 | 7000 | 5000 |
| Maintenance | 9000 | 12000 | (3000) |
| Consumables | 6000 | 4000 | 2000 |
| Plant services | 20000 | 21000 | (1000) |
| etc. | etc. | etc. | etc. |
| Total plant support costs | 6000 | 57000 | 3000 |
| Contribution from extra sales | 100000 | 85000 | (15000) |
| Cash flow | 40000 | 28000 | (12000) |

Brackets denote unfavourable variances.

first specified ? Have there been unexpected changes in costs? Does the valume of output and sales differ from forecasts? Have the budgeted margins been achieved? All the ingredients of revenue and cost within the original calculation are scrutinised and deviations noted.

A Project audit also has a systems aspect. Is the information system the same which furnished the original date? For instance, has the term 'departmental efficiency' the precise meaning as before? Have all the assumptions been confirmed? Consider, as an illustration, all the differences between a predicted three-shift and an actual two-shift system. Have there been cost apportionments which blur the incremental analysis? Are there any operational aspects which will require subsequent provisions, such as extra maintenance spares, or affected the expected plant life?

The result of the audit will be a report, This is more effective if it comes in a standard format. If convenient, different forms can be used for projects above or below a key value, thus reflecting different levels of scrutiny. The report summarises the main audit findings and recommendations and highlights the key points of the financial summary. Wherever possible, financial comparisons should be in constant terms, *i.e.*, inflation effects should be segregated.

To illustrate a simple form of audit summary consider Example 1 in Chapter 8 (p. 138). Assume that it is a year after the scheduled start-up date. Plant construction costs came to £110000, project completion was delayed by a month and subsequent commissioning difficulties reduced the volume of saleable output expected for the first year of operation. Table 10.1a shows part of a revised cost and revenue computation which yields the cash flow for the year. In the light of this experience, future cash flows are now expected to be reduced by 10 % over the remainder of the plant life. Table 10.1b

TABLE 10.1b

**Audit Return Computation**

| *Year* | *Forecast cash flow* (£) | *Revised cash flow* (£) | *Variance* (£) |
|---|---|---|---|
| 0 | (100000) | (110000) | (10000) |
| 1 | 40000 | 28000 | (12000) |
| 2 | 30000 | 27000 | (3000) |
| 3 | 30000 | 27000 | (3000) |
| 4 | 25000 | 22500 | (2500) |
| 5 | 25000 | 22500 | (2500) |
| DCF return | 16.8% | 5.2% | (11.6%) |

indicates the effect this will have on project returns. It will be seen from the outcome comparison that the excess capital expenditure together with the reduced benefit cash flow has a big effect on the project return.

### *The Audit Yield*

To some extent this has already been anticipated when the case for a project audit was put. It is, however, useful to list its main benefits, and these should be seen in the context of on going operations and not as the result of an isolated activity.

1. The audit helps to clarify the need for remedial measures. These may be operational changes or additional projects.
2. It may reinforce the case for technical/design changes with future similar plant.
3. It might make a firm more circumspect about the industrial relations and productivity bargaining aspects of a new project.
4. Future project preparation might become more rigorous with greater scrutiny of assumptions.
5. Even if everything has gone well, the project audit is a point of departure for plant performance improvement and cost reduction schemes.

## The Practice of Outcome Evaluation

Project audits are a sensitive and generally a confidential matter. This may well be why so relatively little is published about the subject. The most systematic study about its nature and prevalence has been carried out by Luder. His investigation was into investment control, of which the audit is a part, and in this he had the cooperation of thirty-eight companies. Of these twenty-five were US firms; the remainder were German companies. Nineteen out of the twenty-five US companies and five out of the thirteen German companies had an investment project control and follow-up system. The difference between the two sets of firms is significant and is accented by the fact that the five German firms included subsidiaries of US companies.

Luder found that much of the available information, being obtained initially for other purposes, was not the most appropriate for control requirements, nor was it always of the necessary quality. With most companies there was no systems evaluation focused on the furnishing of such data. Where it was available it often did not lead to corrective action. The relative shortage of suitable staff left most of the control data with the original project estimators and, whilst this had a learning function, it eroded the discipline of a separate audit.

Rockley[2] has provided some evidence of project follow-up systems in British industry. Some firms which do have a system apply it after, say, the first year of plant operation and from this make assumptions about the overall project outcome for the remainder of the plant life. The horizon of the plant proposal is not matched by an equal time scale of retrospect. This does not mean, of course, that the firm ceases to collect data about its production plant; it will do so at the operational purposes, rather than for a time interval series of project audits. The need to gather particular information for special purposes is likely to remain. However, these no longer form part of the investment process.

### *Some Case Examples*

Company A, in the engineering industry, had considered a formal project audit system but thought there were too many variables for detailed economic evaluation. Nevertheless, there was verification of specified project objectives, such as increased production rates or reduced manning levels. In that respect the original project applicants could and were held responsible for meeting such claims.

In its policy and procedure statements for capital expenditure, company C specifisd the follow-up investigation to be carried out by the management accounting department to ensure that anticipated savings had materialised where projects had in the first place been approved on a financial basis. Where the anticipated savings had not been achieved details of remedial action had to be submitted. Follow-up investigations had to be initiated three months after the physical project completion.

A separate follow-up procedure applied to small projects with above-average financial viability. The project procedure was confined here to proposals with a pay-off period of one year or less and where the cost savings were due to a reduction in labour or revenue expenditure costs. It did not apply to capacity expansion projects. The follow-up was scheduled to commence at the end of the pay-off period. The follow-up report was made on a special form, designed to highlight the manner of anticipated saving. For instance, it required a detailed statement of labour savings with the results alongside the estimates. Where the project did not achieve the expected savings, the capital sum was withdrawn from the special authorisation procedure and debited to the appropriate capital expenditure budget.

In company D the project review was part of the standard accounting procedure and was, in the first instance, concerned with variances in the capital costs against budget. The anticipated savings and additional revenue expenses, such as plant maintenance, had to be built into cost standards and thus provided project feedback in operating terms. Depending on their nature, expenditure reviews were the responsibility of either the divisional controllers or the group management accountant. For projects over a certain size the reviews were scheduled to take place:

1. Twelve months after the estimated commissioning date and twelve months from the actual commissioning date if more than three months later.

2. After that when any break-even point was scheduled to be met.
3. Again when full plant capacity was estimated to have been reached.

The review reports were circulated to all the original signatories and authorities to the original capital project form. The internal audit department was required in the normal course of its activities to audit some of these post-compeletion reviews. The review system reflected the company's evolution towards a fully-integrated planning and control system. Review experience was expected to affect targets for subsequent capital projects. Failures to meet targets would increase the required percentage returns.

It was a prime responsibility of the finance division staff to ensure that reports and action followed these reviews at the appropriate levels.

**Check List: Project Audit**

*First Review*

1. Has the project been completed within its authorised expenditure? If not, why not?
2. Was the project completed on time? If not, what were the reasons?
3. Is there a standard practice of plant handover?
4. Does the installed plant work?
5. Was plant commissioning within budget and time schedule?
6. Did licensors, suppliers and contractors fulfil their commissioning obligations?
7. Has all the plant been accepted?
8. Where plant has proved unsatisfactory have any monies been retained, any redress sought?

9. What were the greatest commissioning problems, surprises?
10. Does the plant work to design and operating specifications?
11. Did operating procedures have to be changed because of commissioning experience? What effects will this have on costs, efficiencies?
12. Was operator and supervisory training adequate?
13. Have any unexpected safety hazards come to light? If so, what is being done about them?
14. What industrial relations problems have been encountered and what lessons have been drawn for future projects?

*The Main Performance Audit*

15. Who should carry this out? Why?
16. When should it be undertaken?
17. What documentation exists for project audits?
18. Has the plant kept its performance promise in terms of efficiency, production rates, cost standards?
19. Have the expected manning levels been achieved? If not what are the major problems?
20. Have product sales predictions materialised?
21. Have the project cash flows met forecasts?
22. What are the reasons for cash flow variances?
23. Have product quality standards been achieved?
24. What contingent problems or losses have been discovered?
25. What use is made of audit reports to help future projects?

## REFERENCES

1. Luder, K., *Investitionskontrolle*, Betriebswirtschaftlicher Verlag Dr. Th Gabler, (Wiesbaden, 1969).

2. Rockley, L.E., *Capital Investment Decisions*, Business Books Ltd,, (London, 1968).

# 11

# ORGANISATIONAL DESIGN FOR DEVELOPMENT PROJECTS

ASHOK PRADHAN*

Development planning has been in practice in the developing countries for more than thirty years now. For almost two decades, however, the stress has been on 'economic growth' as the basic content of planning. It was thought that with the size of the 'cake' growing bigger the socio-economic problems would be automatically taken care of, A heavy dose of capital input was considered to be the sufficient cause for economic

*Mr. Ashok Pradhan is Director in the Department of Personnel and Administrative Reforms, Government of India, New Delhi.

This paper was presented at the Regional Programme on "Administrative Planning and Implementation of Development Projects" conducted jointly by UN Asian and Pacific Development Centre, Department of Personnel and Administrative Reforms, Government of India and the Indian Institute of Public Administration in New Delhi (May 18—June 4, 1981). The author is grateful to Messrs. Hyder Ali (Bangladesh). Ghulam Dastagir Amami (Afghanistan), Shaik Mowla (India), Ahmed Puat I. Nordin (Malaysia), A.N. Bhattarai (Nepal), Jayasinghe Arachchige Ariyasena (Sri Lanka) and Mrs. Soisamorn Poonyasawat of Thailand for their suggestions in the preparation of this paper.

growth and social justice. It was simultaneously assumed that skills and expertise in the form of organisations and personnel necessary for development effort either already existed or would automatically grow during the life-cycle of a development project presenting no problems in project formulation, operation and implementation.

The recent history, however, belies these assumptions. Whatever 'economic growth' has taken place, it has not brought about social justice in the form of upliftment of the poor and distribution of incomes. There has been a conspicuous absence of organisations compatible with the content and character of development planning. However, it is now being increasingly realised that there has been utter lack of administrative planning as an element of development planning for formulation of plans, programmes and projects and for providing necessary organisational skills for the operation and implementation of the projects. A number of U.N. agencies have confirmed that there is "acute shortage of good and well prepared projects and of suitable organisational structure which were the major impediments to the execution of plans for development."[1]

Planning and organisation are inseparable arms of national development effort. "On the one hand, (national) development planning is an organised effort; the result of planning depends heavily on how well it is organised. On the other hand, planning is a part of the administrative process of modern complex organisation or organisational system. The common feature of modern organisation and development planning is rationality and objective."[2] Undoubtedly development planning involves the setting up of modern organisation for economic development. Thus, there is no denying the fact that organisation building is an integral part of the planning process.

However, it is necessary for any developing economy to be able to evolve an organisation suited to its genius which at the same time is capable of achieving the objectives of development projects. The issues which need to be examined are therefore as to what sort of organisations have so far been tried in the development effort; what has been the experience; whether these have been able to deliver the goods; if not, the reasons therefore; and what are the weaknesses of the traditional organisational set up in the developing countries which have been most of the time responsible for implementing development projects.

As the entire gamut of development effort in the developing countries could be sizeable, an attempt has been made in this paper to limit the area of inquiry to the rural development projects adopted by some countries in the Asian region.

### *Characteristics of Development Projects*

As indicated above, a development project is basically different in content and character from normal projects. It is "an implicit or explicit statement of social change"—an instrument to achieve goals of development planning.

Development project is also defined sometimes as a proposal for capital investment which could result in production, exploitation of resources or development of socio-economic infrastructure. It is further conceived as a compilation of data which should enable appraisal to be made of the economic benefit and disadvantages attendant upon allocation of resources for the production ofgoods and services. Thus, it is clear that a development project does not aim only at creating and delivering goods and services to a target group or in a particular area but basically it aims at bringing about behavioural change ultimately leading to social change. Hence, it is not enough to consider and examine the economic aspects of planning, *i.e.*, input and output ratio, rate of return, etc.; it is also necessary to ensurethat the plan and implementation thereof bring about the desired social change. A development project further envisages a definite relationship between administrative apparatus/organisation and the beneficiaries. It is considered necessary that there is participation of the beneficiary groups and identification of their needs with the national planning objectives to incorporate them in the development projects designed for their benefit.

Development projects are usually of two types: one—infrastructure construction project with social change as its implicit/subsidiary goal. For example, construction of an ordinary irrigation channel project could lead to change in the life styles of beneficiaries. The availability of irrigation facilities could lead to double cropping or multiple cropping pattern thereby necessitating new inputs in the form of seeds and fertilizers. The activities so generated would not only bring about economic improvement, but would also lead to consequent social change.

The other—non-infrastructure projects in the rural sector—be exemplified by nutrition programme, famine relief, health and family welfare, educational facilities, etc. Here, explicitly the basic objective is to bring about social change. For example, the objective of the educational programmes may be to change the critical behavioural pattern of the rural populace by creating an awareness that education for girls is potentially useful. The educated girls in turn would automatically cause changes in the life style of the rural masses.

*Country Description of Organisational Patterns*

A bird's eye view of development projects in the countries selected for study, *viz.*, Bangladesh, Afghanistan, Sri Lanka, Nepal, Thailand, Malaysia and India reveals that the most prevalent pattern is the basic hierarchical structure. With reference to the scope of the study, *i.e.*, the rural development, the *Bangladesh* pattern relies on a hierarchical administrative organisation. The headquarters of Integrated Rural Development Project financed by IDA has been set up in the national capital. The organisation is headed by a Director General who is assisted by an Executive Director responsible for a project area and other directors dealing with Cooperation, finance, Loan and Recovery of Loan, and Training. In the

Project area, there is a Project Director and a Deputy Project Director with staff support at the district level and a Project Officer and a Deputy Project Officer with supporting staff at thana level.

There is yet another organisational set up. For administrative purposes the whole area of Bangladesh is divided into four divisions and each Division is administratively headed by a Commissioner. A Divisional Development Board has been set up which has been given some financial allocation to take up development projects. The Board is headed by a Minister and the Commissioner acts as the Secretary. Members of Parliament within the Division and all the Deputy Commissioners are members of this Board.

At the thana level there is a Thana Council headed by the subdivisional officer. All the Chairmen of the Union Council are its members. There is also a Thana Development Board which recommends the projects to be taken up for implementation to the Thana Council. All the elected chairmen of the Union Councils are its members and they also execute the projects with finances provided by the government.

In respect of *Afghanistan*, the new Five Year plan for expansion of education at primary and middle school level was examined. Keeping in view the priority accorded to education by Afghan Government, a new comprehensive curriculum has been designed and the system of education changed from 1-12 to 1-10. In order to achieve literacy/education as an input for achieving national socio-economic goals, tex, books have been introduced in Edifferent languages. The apex body is the Ministry of Education under the charge of a Minister who is assisted by two Deputy Ministers who in turn, control 16 departments within the Ministry. At organisational level there is a Provincial Director of Education with requisite-staff; their primary goal is to establish a number of new primary schools and to upgrade a number of village schools to primary and middle school levels. Even though a number of schools are in the government owned buildings there are a lot of schools, particularly at the primary level in mosques and rented buildings. The thrust it now on providing proper buildings to the schools and to ensure that education reaches free of cost and without discrimination to all sections of people—both male and female. It would be seen that the organisational pattern is traditional and hierarchical and a number of levels are involved in decision making. At the grass root level, in spite of clear objectives there are bottlenecks in terms of rules and regulations and slow decision making process.

In *Sri Lanka*, a development project for housing was examined. An autonomous body, namely, National Housing Development Authority has before it the objective of constructing 1,50.000 houses all over the island within four years for housing low income group people including the rural poor. The Authority's organisation has three main divisions: Administrative Planning and Policy, Finance and Construction, each under one Deputy General Manager. They are, in turn, assisted by Assistant General Managers in charge of different branches. Overall control (responsibility and authority) is, however, exercised by the General Manager of the Authority. Most of the policy decisions are taken by the General Manager with the assistance of lower level officers. Mostly, construction, preparation of different types of housing plans, raw material availability are also discussed by these officers once a month. The authority has been set up to get rid of slow government procedures and to ensure that the project proceeds fast and meets its targets in time.

In *Nepal*, an effort has been made to dissociate development administration from local regulatory agencies at the district level and below. Under the Ministry responsible for development, the Local Development Officer has been named as Chief Coordinator, as developmental activities are being handled at district level by officers drawn from different departments like agriculture, industry, irrigation, etc. At the village level there is an institution of 'Gram Panchayat of which 'Gram Karyakarta' is the

Secretary. Gram Karyakarta is not an official but one of the villagers picked up for motivating the villagers to articulate their needs and to match them with development projects. He works as eyes and ears of Local Development Officer, besides motivating the villagers; he reports back the reaction of the common villagers eo a development project. The strength of the system, it is felt, is in the institution of the Gram Karyakàrtas who are in constant touch with the intended beneficiaries of development project and are vehicles of communication between the officers and the beneficiaries. These efforts do result in proper identification of their needs and formulation of projects based thereon. However, the experience and practice has been that all the ills of functional organisation are very much in evidence and problems of communication, coordination and delay in decision making, etc., still persist.

The *Thai* development pattern is a little different. The entire country is divided into 71 provinces each headed by a Governor who is, by and large, under the office of Under Secretary of State, Ministry of Interior. There are districts headed by district level officers and below the district are the basic units, *i.e.*, the village. Both the districts and provinces, in matters of development, are under the Central Administration. They receive policy directives, rules and regulations from the departments, ministries and cabinet, to implement effectively within their jurisdiction.

Since the unit of a district is small and only limited number of villages are under it, people's participation is being evidenced and needs of the people are being served as there is identification between the needs of the people and the national plan priorities.

In *Malaysia*, a model of bifurcation of different development activities under autonomous corporations under the overall supervision of Ministry of Public Enterprises is under way. A large number of autonomous corporations have been set up to deal with the rural development, namely credit facilities, distribution of seeds, fertilizers, etc. An attempt has been made to hasten the decision making process and to avoid too many levels. For example, National Rice and Paddy Board has been set up as an agency for fixing minimum price of rice and paddy in order to provide price support to the farmers and to save them from the exploitation of the middlemen. The organisation also makes spot purchases at the minimum fixed price to avoid distress sales at lower price by the farmer. In spite of these laudable objectives and clear cut organisational set up for achieving a definite goal, at times the Corporation has not been able to deliver the goods.

In *India*, the first development effort was articulated through community development projects. The entire apparatus for community development was started under the supervision of the district officers. It was, however, felt from the mid-50s onwards that for development purposes a separate pattern should be evolved. Emphasis was first laid on the Panchayati Raj institutions, the basic features of which were the threetier system in which the village, the block and the district levels were focal points in planning and execution of development projects. The concept of zila parishad/district board under the control and supervision of an elected representative having a senior civil servant as Secretary or the Chief Executive Officer has gradually evolved particularly in the state of Maharashtra, Gujarat, Andhra Pradesh and Rajasthan. There are of course, minor variations. In some states, district level parishad is the apex body/nodal agency for project formulation and supervision of execution of projects. whereas in other states it is the samiti at the block level which is the main body for formulation and execution of development projects, while the district body only takes policy decisions. These are broadly the Maharashtra, Gujarat and Rajasthan patterns which have gradually percolated to the states with minor variations.

The basic objective of the Panchayati Raj institution was to enlist participation of the beneficiaries of the programme and to involve them in decision making. However, it has been noted by experts that Panchayati Raj institutions act as "gate keeper" and prevent the flow of benefits to the weaker sections of the rural community as they are dominated by rich and powerful vested interest groups. The participation of targeted beneficiary group more often than not results in the non-participation of the "other" non-benefiting sections of rural community who dispay their resistance in both civil and not so civil a manner.[3]

Yet another important feature of rural development seen in India is the proliferation of special programmes accompanied by special project organisations. Programmes like DPAP, SFDA, IADP and CAD have thus built-in project organisations. The speciai organisations around the programmes have a nucleus staff but they depend mostly on regular line department for execution of projects. Experience shows that this kind of project organisation has neither the planning skill nor the implementation machinery, "These organisations exist for funding purposes mainly and often find it hard to get their work done through the regular departments which do not like to submit the themselves to the discipline of project organisation. In consequence, the project set up tends to become ad island unto itself. It does not mesh up with larger organisational outfit at the field level and cannot become very effective as a result. Special agencies are created to achieve definite results but in practice these hardly work that way. The accent is more on expenditure than getting results within a time horizon."[4]

*Common Organisational Patterns in Government—Types, Features and Weaknesses*

It is obvious from that foregoing that a mixture of patterns has evolved in the developing countries in the region to deal with and implement development projects. The most common of them all is the existing traditional hierarchical pattern in which rules, regulations, accountability and multiplicitly of levels play an important role. Realising these points as weaknesses and not being compatible with the demands of a development project, the governments in the region have introduced and experimented with new types of organisations.

These organisations include Panchayati Raj institutions (India and Nepal), and special project organisations for special rural (and other) programmes, such as IADP, CAD, etc.

Yet another type is the autonomous bodies created by government as public sector undertakings. It can be departmental undertakings under a ministry, statutory corporations created by an Act of the legislature (India, Malaysia, Ceylon, etc.) and government companies registered under the Compainies Act. The examples are Railways, SAIL, BHEL, Sindri Fertilizer in India and MARA, FELDA, UDA in Malaysia.

However, in spite of the varying degrees of success which these organisations have met in different countries, the basic trend in all these patterns seems to be "replication" of existing government bureaucratic hierarchical patterns. The weaknesses of all these patterns and designs continue to be the multiplicity of levels, formal and slow communication, diffused responsibility, slow decision making and lack of clear cut responsibility leading to insularity. Despite efforts, the participation of beneficiaries has been ephemeral and hardly meaningful. Compelling requirements of technical knowledge gave led to the inclusion or association of experts with the organisation; but integration, and assimilation has not taken place thus defeating the very purpose of an organisation. There has been, on the other hand, a wide gap between precept and practise and an unnecessary controversy about the role of a specialist in the organisation, *vis-a-vis* the generalist.

It is thus clear that the pattern has not been compatible with and conducive to the goal of social change—the basic purpose of a development project. There is no doubt that change is *sine qua non* in order to meet the objectives of a development project. The necessity of reducing levels, frank and smooth communication, clear cut responsibility, and reasonable use of rules and regulations is thus very clear. It is thus important that an organisation does not become an end in itself but continues to be a means to the ends of a development project.

What are the alternatives? Here we can identify three patterns, (a) traditional functional type of organisation, (b) projectised organisation, and (c) matrix organisation. A word about each of them is necessary here.

The traditional organisational structure is known as hierarchical/functional organisation This is thestandard pyramid type with top management at the top of the chart and middle and lower management spreading out down the pyramid. The organisation is broken down into different functional units, such as engineering, research, accounting, administration. The structure is obviously based on management theories, such as specialisation, line and staff relations, authority and responsibility, and span of control. The major functional sub-units are staffed by disciplines like engineering or accounting, according to the doctrine of specialisation. It is considered easier to manage specialists if they are grouped together and if the department head has training and experience in that particular discripline.

The strength of the organisation is in its centralisation of similar resources.

The weakness of the functional organisation are the converse of its strength. When a functional organisation is concerned with multiple projects, conflicts invariably arise over the relative priorities of different projects in the competition for resources. A functional department based on a technical speciality often places more emphasis on its own speciality rather than the goals of the project. Lack on motivation and inertia are other problems hindering fulfilment of goals.

The opposite of the hierarchical/ functional organisation is the single purpose project organisation. In a projectised organisation all the resources necessary for the accomplishment of a specific objective are reparated from the regular functional structure and the project is set up as a self-contained unit headed by a Project Manager. The Project Manager is given considerable authority over the project and may acquire resources from either inside or outside the overall organisation. All the personnel on the project are under the direct authority of the Project Manager for the duration of the project. In effect a large organisation sets up a smaller, temporary and special purpose structure for the accomplishment of a specific objective. It is interesting to note that the internal structure of the project organisation is functional. That is, the project team is divided into various functional areas.

While the projects can be managed by all the three (functional, projectised and matrix) types of organisational structures, the advantages of the project organisation flow from the singleness of purpose and unity of command. An *espirit de corps* is developed through the clear understanding of and focus on the single objective. Informal communication is effective in a close knit team. Project Manager has all the necessary resources under his direct control.

However, to assume that project organisation is a perfect solution to all project management problems would be incorrect Setting up a new and highly temporary structure upsets the regular organisation. There is also duplication of facilities and inefficient use of resources. Another serious problem with the project organisation is the question of job security upon termination of temporary project. Often the project personnel lose their "home" in the functional structure while they are off on the project.

The functional/hierarchical organisation is organised around technical inputs, such as engineering and marketing. The project organisation is a single purpose structure organised around project outputs, such as a new dam or a new product. Both of these are unidimensional in structure in a multidimensional world. The problem in each of these organisational structures is how to get a proper balance between the long-term objectives of functional departments in building technical expertise and the short-term objectives of the project.

The third type of organisation, namely, the matrix organisation is a multi-dimensional structure that tries to maximise the strengths and minimise the weaknesses of both the project and the functional structures. The matrix organisation combines the standard vertical hierarchical structure with a superimposed lateral or horizontal structure of a project coordinator.

The major benefits of the matrix organisation are the balancing of objectives, the coordination across functional department lines, and the visibility of the project objectives through the project coordinator' office. The major disadvantage in a matrix set up is that the man in the middle is working for two bosses. Vertically he reports to his functional department head; horizontally he reports to the project coordinator or project manager. In a conflict situation he can be caught in the middle.

The project manager often feels that he has little authority with regard to the functional department. On the other hand, the functional department head often feels that the project coordinator is interfering in his territory. The solution to the problem perhaps lies in clearly defining the roles, responsibility and authority of each of the actors. The project coordinator specifies what is to be done and the functional department is responsible for how it is to be done.

Experience has, however, shown that there is no one particular approach that is perfect for all situations. The best solution is perhaps contingent upon the key factors in the environment in which the project will have to operate. A list of key factor would help us to choose the right organisational structure for the given conditions on a specific project with a given organisation and particular environment.

*Common Issues in Organisational Patterns*

While it is true that no single type of organisation can be suggested is a panacea for all the organisational ills of development projects, some common issues alling the organisational systems in most of the developing countries can be identified:

*1. Structural Issues*

As stated earlier, most of the development organisation models tried in developing countries are the "replication" of the traditional hierarchical organisation. Hence, they also suffer from multiplicity of levels resulting in slow decision making. The communication pattern is formal, impersonal and impeded affecting as well the quality of coordination within the organisation and individuals and agencies outside with which it has to interact. The lack of delegation of authority and too steep a hierarchy result in demotivating the personnel. The achievement of the goal of the organisation no longer stirs them to responsible action. Diffused responsibility, overemphasis on rules, regulations and greater stress on accountability, therefore, sap the organisation of the dynamism and forward looking attitude which is so very necessary for development projects.

*2. Procedural Issues*

It is generally recognised that various functionaries of an organisation in developing countries lack necessary knowledge, expertise and skills. There is acute shortage of qualified and experienced personnel for storage, retrieval and appraisal of data and information. Consequently, it is found difficult not only to effectively perform some of the day-to-day functions of the organisation, but lack of some skills makes it almost impossible to have a meaningful review and appraisal of the project activities.

The personned are more often than not prisoners of rules, regulations and procedures, which are given precedence over other important project activities to the detriment of project interests. The commitment to rules, regulations and procedures also makes the organisation such that the beneficiaries of the project rarely get a participative role. A donor-recipient relationship comes to stay between the project authorities and the beneficiaries.

Increased use of technology has made the role of specialists very important in the project organisation. Due to faulty personnel policies and clash of group interests, specialist *vs.* generalist conflict has come to the fore even at the cost of the project.

*3. Implementation Capability of a Development Organisation*

Due to structural and personnel problems characterising the development organisations, as indicated above, the implementation process of a development project-gets impeded. The emphasis and priority generally accorded to rules and procedures adversely affect commitment and sense of urgency towards realisation of objectives of the project.

The delay in turn disturbs the sequence of other development projects which might have been linked with or dependent upon the output of the delayed project.

*Areas for Reform*

It would be futile to suggest any uniform or all-embracing measures for improvement of a development organisation, *per se*, as the organisational pattern for a development project operating at national or state level is bound and ought to be different from the one at village or block level. One has also to take into consideration the nature, character, location and environment of a project while suggesting any measures. However, considering the problems faced by development projects, one can think of a few areas which are common to all development projects, for bringing about improvement. These may relate to structural personnel and procedural matters. It is common knowledge that the multi-level, hierarchically ordained bureaucratic system of organisation is totally unsuited for development administration. The traditional structure of bureaucracy being an integral part of the political process and the social system, one cannot bring about drastic structural changes in the bureaucratic system without effecting corresponding changes in the political and social systems. This being so, it is unrealistic to assume that any specially designed structure of a project organisation can remain totally unaffected by the characteristics of the traditional system of bureaucracy. Nevertheless, attempts can be made to bring about certain changes in the structure of the development projects. Firstly, the structure should be so designed as to provide minimum number of hierarchical levels so that the pace of decision making process may be accelerated. This will not only help cut down delays in the execution of the projects, but speed up the process of distribution of benefits to the target groups Secondly, the roles and responsibilities of the functionaries should not only be clearly defined but should also be accompanied by adequate power to make the functionaries responsive to the requirements and goals of the organisation. Thirdly, communication being the necessary vehicle by which employees' activities are coordinated and directed towards the goals of the organisation, it assumes great significance in a development project, the more so when projects are functioning in a time-frame with specified targets to achieve. Smoother and informal communication as supplement to formal channel of communication will not only improve the functioning within the organisation, but will also help provide coordination and communication with the intended beneficiaries. Fourthly, the organisation structure should provide for information sharing in that the project authorities come to know, what is the exact nature of the environment in which the project is operating, which of the project activities are being vigorously pursued, and which of them are deviating from the targets, thereby needing corrective measures at the appropriate time, etc. The project managers should also establish project evaluation and monitoring units and design systems which are capable of controlling the emergent problems.

Concomitant to the changes in the organisation structure is the need for developing the personnel. Needless to say, a team of trained and skilled personnel is as important for a development project organisation as other inputs like finances, machinery, etc. It is increasingly felt that in an organisation of development project, task orientation or target phenomena should be one of the foremost considerations, providing as it should, a clear-cut direction and goal to the project functionaries. The task or output orientation works back from the results, provides for productivity measurement and performance auditing thereby leading to increase in efficiency signifying either a reduction in cost or cut in delays. Obviously, this will necessitate greater professionalisation among the project personnel by imparting knowledge and skill to apply various tools and techniques of management to enable them to make rational decisions, especially in the critical areas of resource allocation and utilisation. Another important factor in personnel development is the attitudinal changes to be brought about among the functionaries so that they become more and more responsive to the needs and aspirations of the people for whom the projects are intended. Developing group norms and creating an atmosphere of mutual trust and cooperation which also provides for maximum involvement of the project personnel in the decision making process in the organisation is yet another factor that needs to be encouraged. These can be achieved through continuous and carefully designed training programmes which should be made an integral part of the organisational system itself.

In the context of development projects, excessive reliance on rules and procedures often leads to inordinate delay in the execution of the programmes, thereby causing hardships to the beneficiaries by denying them the fruits of development. It is, therefore, essential that efforts are made to have a fresh look at the rules, regulations and procedures with a view to simplifying them to suit the developmental goals. Certain amount of flexibility in the application of rules is also necessary to make the delivery system more effective.

It would thus be seen that the changes suggested in the structural, personnel and procedural matters would greatly help enhance the implementation capability of the development projects. The implementation capability of a project is largely determined how best the three parameters of project management *viz.*, time, cost and performance are met while pursuing the targets. In this, the creative, flexible and innovative approach of the project manager becomes all the more important. He should ensure that the project personnel concern themselves more with the implementation of the project rather than getting bogged down with the routine administrative statistical exercises about the progress appraisal of the project. The performance of the project personnel should legitimately be measured not in terms of the audit objections, but on the successful completion of the project within the time-cost parameters. More importantly, the project functionaries should make every effort to involve the beneficiaries at the grass root level in the organisation so as to be able to align the project with the needs and aspirations of the target groups. Ultimately, it is on the people's participation that the success or failure of a project depends.

## REFERENCES

1. United Nations, Organisational Systems for National Planning, ST/ESA/SERE/18, p. 107.
2. *Ibid.*
3. Report of the Working Group on Block Level Planning (Mimeo.) Planning Commission, Government of India, 1978, Chapter 6.
4. Mohit Bhattacharya, "Administrative and Organisation Issues in Rural Development," The Indian Journal of Publice Administration, Oct.-Dec. 1978. Vol. XXIV, No. 4, p. 1173.

## BIBLIOGRAPHY

1. Adelman, Irma *(et al.)*, *Economic Growth and Social Equity in Developing Countries*, Stanford University Press, 1973.

2. Bhattacharya, Mohit, 'Administrative and Organisational Issues in Rural Development', *The Indian Journal of Public Administration*, Vol. XXIV—No. 4, p. 1173.

3. Dayal, Ishwar and Dayal, Amrit Kala, *Organisation for Management in Developing Countries*, Delhi, Concept, 1978.

4. Dubhashi, P.R., 'Organisation Building', *The Indian Journal of Public Administration*, January—March, 1980, Vol. XXVI—No. 1, p. 50.

5. Hirschman, Albert O., *The Strategy of Economic Development*, New Haven, Yale University Press. 1960.

6. Laxmi Narain, *Principles and Practice of Public Enterprise Management*, New Delhi, S. Chand Co., 1980.

7. Planning Commission, Government of India, *Report of the Working Group on Block Level Planning (Mimeo.)*, Chapter 6, 1978.

8. Saxena, A.P. (*Ed*), *Administrative Reforms for Decentralized Development*, Kuala Lampur, Asian and Pacific Development Administration Centre, 1980.

9. United Nations, *Organisational Systems for National Planning*, ST/ESA/SERE/18, p. 107.

# 12

# PROJECT LEADERSHIP AND CONTROL

## Introduction

Effective leadership is not the product of certain personality traits as much as it is a set of skills and attitudes appropriate to a given situation. It is not possible to divide people into "leaders" and "followers" by rigid characterizations. An individual who is clearly a subordinate in one situation may be acclaimed by his group as their leader in another.

Most people who reach positions of supervision and management in data processing were originally hired for an entirely different set of skills, technical ones. When there is an opening for a group leader, the most technically expert person is often appointed to it. On the face of it, this is not particularly rational because the skills required are not the same. But it is what people expect; most technicians would rather work for a supervisor whose technical skill they admire. As long as that attitude prevails, anyone in a management position in data processing who knows little about computers and has not proved himself as a technician will have difficulty in commanding the respect of his subordinates.

Some, promoted analysts and programmers become good supervisors, while others do not. As has already been said, the difference is less in their personalities than in their attitudes and supervisory skills. There are no hard-and-fast rules for becoming an effective supervisor. The diversities of human behaviour are almost infinite, and every situation is unique. It is possible to set out useful principles and guidelines, however, and that is the purpose of this chapter.

A good way to begin is to define two extreme styles of leadership. One is task-oriented and the other is people-oriented. A task-oriented manager sees his job as one of achieving work goals. He is formal and reserved; that is, he maintains a psychological distance between himself and his staff. He relies on job descriptions and standard procedures, and judges people by their work performance, often being critical. He delegates work often and generally gives people a free rein, but he expects that they will make mistakes and he plans accordingly. The people-oriented manager is relaxed, warm, and friendly. He bases his evaluations of people on how well he likes them, and tends to run his group along democratic lines. He does not delegate very often, and supervises his staff more closely. As opposed to the task-oriented manager, he is psychologically close to his people, "one of the boys." Perhaps the reader will recognize himself or a past or present boss in one of these descriptions.

A totally task-oriented manager is probably not well liked by his staff; he is the type they describe as "a cold bastard." An extremely people-oriented manager is rarely well liked either; he is too hearty, too "buddy-buddy." His staff finds it difficult to look up to him when he places himself on their level all the time, and because he is not task-oriented he rarely managers to get any actual work done. An ideal manager could be described as one who combines task orientation with people orientation, and finds an appropriate balance in the middle. The human relations school of management that came into full flower following the Hawthorne experiments overstressed the importance of people orientation. This was partly an overreaction to the extreme authoritarian management as it was exercised previously. It is now recognized that this approach needs some correction; psychologically distant managers are more effective.

With these concepts as background, we will examine from a practical standpoint the kinds of activities a project leader engages in. In this chapter, the emphasis is on people-oriented behaviour. The subjects covered here are: getting started, planning work, decision making, giving orders, setting goals, giving support, delegating, criticizing, praising and rewarding, settling grievances, and educating and training.

**Initiative and Drive**

Let's suppose you have just been made a project leader and your first day in that job will be tomorrow. What should you do? How should you act to be sure of getting off on the right foot? The answer depends in part on whether you are just joining the organization or whether you have been promoted from within. In the latter case, your task is easier in many ways because you know the people and you know what will be expected of you. You have had time to observe other project leaders, and you can use that experience as a guideline for how to act (or how not to act, if the other project leaders are in your opinion not as good as they should be). On the other hand, if you are going to be supervising people who were your equals yesterday and will be your subordinates tomorrow, there are potential problems. It is possible that one or more of those on your team feel that they should have gotten the promotion; or, if you are not careful, you may leave yourself open to accusations of "putting an airs."

If you're a newcomer and don't know the people, the problem is to find out what is expected of a project leader. If you haven't already been told what that is, the first thing to do is to get a copy of the job description and study it, and find out what authority you have and what you don't have. (Remember, however, that what it says in the job description—or even what the boss told you when you went for the job interview—isn't necessarily true.) Your level in the hierarchy of the department is partly determined by how much authority you have. Can you recruit staff and fire them without consulting anyone? Probably not, for most project leaders. If a new employee is being hired for your team, do you have any say in it? Are you required to report on the performance of your staff at regular intervals, and if so, how much weight is your opinion given in determining raises, promotions, etc.? Can you change or waive standard installation procedures? As we will see later, it is important to know these things—overstepping your authority can cause problems.

You also need to find out about the people who will be on the project them, if this is known at the time you join the company. If possible, borrow their records from the personnel department. Also, ask your manager for personality sketches and information about their backgrounds and experience. Don't let yourself be unduly prejudiced by any comments from this source' however; the individual described as a troublemaker may turn out to be your strongest team member, or conversely, "the best programmer we've got" could be a prima donna. Wait and make up your own mind after you know them better.

In a new company, it is better at first to err on the side of being somewhat distant than of being too friendly. If you begin to feel after a few weeks that you are being too aloof, it is much easier to gradually relax and become a little more friendly than it is to get tough after you have been easygoing at first.

If you have been promoted from within, your degree of psychological distance will depend on how friendly you were with the people on your team before. If you were always "one of the guys," went out for a drink after work with them, perhaps had social relationships not associated with work, you cannot suddenly cut off all these contacts. If some of the people on your team are close friends, you may not want to; but in that case, it is necessary to try to keep your social life and work separate. Other people on the team might be resentful if they feel that you have favourites. But do gradually cut down on other social contacts. For example, if it has been a custom for everybody to meet around the corner for a few drinks on Friday night, arrive a little later and leave a little sooner than in the past. and skip it altogether once in a while.

If you are entitled to a few status symbols because of your job, accept them, *but only if others with equal status do it too.* In some organizations, it is a "reverse status symbol" to refuse the bigger desk or the new office; don't take privileges other project leaders don't take, even if you are entitled to them. On the other hand, don't refuse them just because you feel funny about it or want to prove what a gooduy you are; there is a chance you might be seen as being patronizing.

Another way to establish that slight but necessary degree of psychological distance is to associate with and act like those who are your equals in status, and those just above you in the hierarchy. This is particularly important if there is the possibility that others may question your right to the job; that is, for example, if you are younger or less experienced than some of the people on your team, and in some organizations (still) if you are female. Being more like those who are your peers may mean, for example, dressing a little bit more conservatively, taking a half-inch off your sideburns, or taking a less flippant attitude toward the company and management.

If you believe that there is a challenge to your right to the job, and if you have the authority to do so, it is sometimes recommended that you start by firing someone. Robert Townsend (see Recommended Readings) says: "Find the worst bad apple in your new barrel and fire him (or her). Any time in the first ninety days will be all right. Don't rush, don't push, and don't have an unnecessary bloodbath."

Some of the things recommended here may offend your life-style. You may feel, for example, that becoming a little more aloof is snobby, or that cutting your their shorter conflicts with your right to express your individuality. If so, it is unfortunate but ture that this kind of thing is necessary. To take just one example: A manager, recently promoted, continued to meet his old pals for a drink after work. He embarrassed them because he had a motorcycle and came into the bar wearing his crash helmet. Eventually, he became the company's laughingstock, and still embarrassed his staff. Some of them had motorcycles, too, but they didn't think it was becoming of their manager to meet them in the bar wearing his helmet, and they would cringe every time he appeared. You must act the way people expect you to act, or you'll never be a successful manager. Business is a game and you don't make the rules for it, at least not yet. You can leave the game if you want, but if you want to play, it's management's game and you've got to play by its rules.

The need to maintain a certain psychological distance, however, doesn't mean you can't be friendly. Be sure to engage in enough of the kind of activity that Dr. Eric Berne (in *Games People Play*: see Recommended Reading) calls "stroking." Stroking is a social ritual whereby you recognize another person's presence. Examples are saying good morning when you meet at the beginning of the day and good night when parting; saying "Have a good weekend" on Friday; asking about vacations, new babies, or hobbies; discussing the weather or the baseball game. For each stroke given, one is expected in return. The content doesn't matter; no real information is exchanged.

There are conventions about the number of strokes to apply to different people on different occasions. For example, when an employee is just back from his vacation, he expects more strokes—a longer conversation—than if you had seen him every day recently, but more from you than from someone he doesn't work with directly. If you omit the expected strokes, perhaps by ignoring a person when you pass him in the corridor, he will begin to worry and feel anxious about what he may have done wrong or why you are angry with him. It is interesting that there are noticeable cultural differences here. In most American companies, one stroke each ("Good morning:" "Good morning") is sufficient for ordinary daily meetings. In England, each person expects two or three strokes, in Italy there may be 30 or 40 required before anyone can get down to business.

**Schedules and Time-frames**

Actual planning of project work will be covered in detail in Part II, but the principles of good planning can be expressed here in a few sentences. First, collect as much information related to the project as possible, remembering that it is never possible to known everything that may be relevant. Take your time; time, care, and thought invested here will pay dividends later on. Try to think of everything that can go wrong, and make contingency plans accordingly. If in doubt, ask your boss or some other experienced person for advice. Another source of guidelines is control documentation from a previous project; choose one that is acknowledged as having been successful. It is not possible to overplan anything, although the plans may be too rigid if no allowances are made for slipups, delays, and changes of course. Finally, document the plans in detail and keep copies for your own use; it can be very in structive at the end of a project to go back to the original schedule to analyze what went wrong and why.

Consult with your staff members during planning, especially with regard to deadlines and objectives that they will have to meet. Once the overall plan is fixed, it may be possible to delegate some of the detailed planning to those who will be carrying out the work; more will be said about delegation in a later section of this chapter.

**Decision Making**

The possible styles of decision making are:

1. Deciding entirely on your own.

2. Consulting with members of the project team first, and then making your own decision.
3. Letting the group decide by consensus or a vote.
4. Delegating the decision to someone else.

The first and the last methods are the fastest ones, and are the methods of choice when there is crisis or pressure and some action must be taken quickly. They are also best for trivial matters not worth sweating over. Methods 2 and 3 are more people-oriented and can be used for important matters that affect everyone in the team. They are also useful when handling thing about which you really have no preference at all and prefer to settle democratically, or when you think you have been too psychologically distant and want to close the gap a little.

Some managers feel that they have to consult their staff about everything, and then delay making up their minds anyway. Gather as much information as is feasible and then decide quickly. You are much more likely to be criticized for being indecisive than for making mistakes. People consistently tend to overestimate their own influence on the boss's decisions, and often think they have been given a suggestion when in fact it was phrased as a direct order. A business organization is not a democracy; don't be afraid to make a decision. Once it is made, however, don't change your mind unless some really fresh information comes to light. One of the most frequent complaints about a poor leader is that he allows himself to be persuaded to change his decision after he has made it.

## Giving Orders

It is very likely that there will be many occasions for a project leader to give direct orders or commands. What "giving orders" is more likely to mean is giving suggestions or instruction. Even when the statement is to be a simple instruction to do something, it is usually much better to phrase it as a request.

Instead of "Drop this on Joe's desk as you go by", say "Would you please. . .?"; or "I'd appreciate it if you would. . . ." The direct command saves more time and may seem to be a hall-mark of efficiency when you're under pressure, but the few extra words *do* make a difference.

When communicating more important decisions, such as that the new standards must be applied, or that everyone's vacation is going to be canceled because the project is behind schedule, it is vital to explain why things have to be this way, You can only hope that you will get your staff to see the logic behind the decision and to see your viewpoint (or management's, if you are passing on an instruction coming from higher up). If you can't, after a reasonable amount of discussion and explanation, it may be necessary to rephrase the orders with a little more directness: "I appreciate those things, but I'm afraid that, for the reasons I've explained, that's the way it's got to be"; or, "I don't like it either, but there's no way we can get it changed."

In this regard, there is nothing wrong in saying that you, too, disagree with an edict from top management (if you really do), as long as in the same breath you express or imply your intention of abiding by it. Pretending that an unpleasant command has come from elsewhere when it was really your idea, or pretending to be against a policy that you secretly agree with, however, is too close to being dishonest. You are lying about your own opinion. Always be absolutely honest in your dealings with your subordinates; if you're not, sooner or later you'll be found out, and they'll lose respect for you and consider you untrustworthy.

### Defining Objectives

Some of the long-term goals may have been already set for the team by the terms of reference for the project. Other goals should be determined in consultation with the individual or the team. When there are team goals to be decided, do it with the whole group in attendance. If you have your own ideas about the details (for example, you want them to finish a report by the end of the month), put it to them as a question ("Can we get it done by the end of the month?"); or, more democratically, give some choice ("We could take anywhere from three weeks to three months over this; what do you think?").

Whenever possible, make the targets graphic and visible. Publish minutes of meetings at which decisions were made. Draw up some kind of wall chart showing the project milestones and put it up over your desk or on the wall in the project room. Colour it in or otherwise indicate progress as work is completed. There is a great deal of satisfaction in being able to see lines or bars of a chart creeping across the sheet day-by-day, and it renews enthusiasm for doing the work that has yet to be done.

When a major milestone is reached, allow the project team the pleasure of some backslapping. This could go as far as celebrating at a special lunch party, or could be merely viewing the charts at the next project meeting and sitting around feeling good.

If a target has been missed, be realistic about it. Encourage people to analyze what went wrong, take corrective action if necessary, and then set a new goal. Be sure that rescheduled targets are reasonable. Continual failure is bad for morale; if there is never any success, people will stop trying. Causes of delay, and their cure and correction, will be discussed in detail in Part II, but it should be pointed out now that overoptimism in setting targets is often to blame. Don't set impossible goals, and try to moderate the team's enthusiasm if they are being too optimistic about their abilities.

**Team Effort Ambience**

Members of the team should be able to feel that the leader is giving them both practical and psychological support. You should be on their side, working with them and for them, helping them whenever possible. This may mean, for example, going to bat for the project team, or for an individual, with management or with users. A "them" versus "us" situation is never desirable, but if intimations of such conflict cannot be avoided, you should be one of "us" if at all possible.

Other ways of giving support are offering constructive criticism to help team members improve their work, arranging for both formal and on-the-job education and training with a view to advancement, and praising and rewarding. These topics are discussed in later sections of this chapter.

**Sharing Responsibility**

As with giving orders, there may not be many occasions for the project leader to delegate responsibility to members of his team. Delegation implies accompaniment of authority to go with it; indeed, the first is useless without the second, but, as was pointed out, a project leader on the first line of management may not have very much authority to delegate. Some opportunities may occur when, for example, there are choices of optional standards to be followed, when estimates are being made and target dates set, or when assignments of staff workers to particular tasks are under consideration.

Delegation of these things does not mean giving your opinion and then asking for the other person's; that is consultation. Delegation is saying, "You decide and inform me afterward." If you really mean to delegate, don't change the decision once it has been made. That turns the situation into a guessing game, with your staff trying to guess what you really want and knowing that no matter what the decision, it will end up as you had secretly determined from the start.

One excellent opportunity for delegation occurs when you go on vacation. Your temporary replacement should always come from below, not from above. It may be standard practice for the data processing manager systems manager, chief programmer, or another project leader to stand in for an absent project leader; if so, fight tooth and nail to get this changed. There must be someone on the team who can run things for a few weeks, and there are always others he can go to for advice if he feels he needs it.

This principle can be extended by appointing someone from the team to stand in for you on other occasions, too. There are a number of ways to arrange it. Team members can be selected in rota, for example, so that if you are away for a few days because of illness or a family emergency, or are working at another company location, whoever is next on the list gets to be "acting project leader." The choice is therefore an arbitrary one and shows that you have no particular favourites. On the other hand, there is a lot to be said for the appointment, official or unofficial, of your second-in-command or right-hand man, who has special project responsibilities while you are there and automatically becomes acting project leader when you aren't. After working with him for a while, you will each know how the other thinks and you will know that he will do things the way you'd like them to be done. It will be business-as-usual while you are gone. Many good managers make point of grooming their successor in this way. Managers who pride themselves on being indispensable are often insecure in their jobs and weak as managers. Remember, if you are indispensable you are also unpromotable. Having someone who could step into your shoes and carry on without disruption increases your chances for promotion the next time the right vacancy occurs.

As a side effect of this policy, you will be giving the opportunity to at least one of the team members to gain more experience and possibly put himself in line for the next project leader vacancy, *and you will be seen to be doing so.* This is one of the ways to give support and demonstrate to the team that you're on their side. There is always the risk that if this approach is entirely successful, you will find your team disappearing out from under you, but it's a risk that must be taken. The alternative is to hold people back in their career progress, or at least not to encourage them, and that would work to the detriment not only of the project, but also of the department and the company.

**Critical Assessment**

Many people hate to criticize and will postpone doing so as long as possible. It's never a pleasant task, and may open the door for bad feelings and hostility. But it is inevitable that there will eventually be a situation where a word of criticism and correction is most definitely called for. The first thing to remember is that when this occurs, the person involved is quite likely to know that he should be criticized, and if you keep putting it off and remain silent, he may lose some respect for you. If you've ever had to teach basic don'ts to a puppy, a kitten, or a young child, you know that it is essential to deliver the spanking or disapproving word as soon after the-act as possible. Not only is it more effective, but it prevents the unnecessary torture of suspense the offender will undergo while waiting. Get it over with quickly, and the air will clear that much sooner.

A second important point is that you should help the person you are criticizing to save face as much as possible. This means having the discussion in private, where there is no chance of being overheard. If he offers excuses or rationalizations, don't demolish them at a stroke. As long as knows what he did wrong and is willing to try to correct it, that is sufficient; don't rub his nose in it. If there are other people involved (for example, perhaps he has done something to anger the boss or the user staff), defend him to them as much as you can, and let him know that it is being done. Even if you chew him up in private, pass over the incident lightly with the third party, denying its importance by your attitude and being soothing. Never, never have a public "court martial" in front of outsiders, or even in the presence of other members of the team.

Third, be constructive in your criticism. "Constructive criticism" is a cliche, the real meaning of which is often neglected. It means offering an alternative and a more approved course of action or behaviour. It means saying, "You did it wrong," and then adding, "This is the way it should be"; or, "I don't like that—don't you think this is better?" As an official rule for the whole project team, this works very well. Potentially unpleasant situations are turned into an objective discussion of the best alternative. In some cases it may be necessary to go further, analyzing what was done wrong, and why, in order to find some way to correct the situation and to prevent its happening again.

**Encouragement and Recognition**

Here is yet another area where the relatively limited status and authority of a project leader must be taken into account. The value of praise as it is seen by the recipient depends on his respect for, and the status of, the person doing the praising. No matter how much a team member likes you and trusts you as a project leader, a resounding "Well done," and a hearty slap on the back may make him wince rather than glow with pride. If he has his doubts about you to start with, this might only make it worse. It is necessary to find more subtle and more acceptable ways of rewarding good work.

Praise is, however, necessary. Do not take the attitude, "Unless I tell you otherwise, you're doing O.K." People need to know where they stand and they like to be told frequently. If you workalongside the team and they have daily opportunities to hear you express your satisfaction about progress, more formal reassurance may not be necessary. The more remote you are and the less they see you, the more important it is to let them know how you feel about their work and the progress of the project. One way to do this is at a weekly team meeting.

Be sure to pass on to an individual, or to the team as a whole, any good words said about them by outsiders. If the user, for example, compliments you on a report that was largely the work of one person, make a special point of telling him about it. And if the most important part of giving criticism is to do it in private, the most important part of praising is to do it in public. Pass on complimentary remarks at the team meeting or in the hearing of the boss If the occasion warrants, go further and get it in writing. When the user is particularly complimentary about an individual's work' ask him to write a memo to your boss about it. If such letters and memos become part of the individual's personnel file, so much the better.

Another more acceptable way of offering praise may be in the form of thanks. If someone has made a special effort or done particularly good work for the project or the team, give him your personal thanks.

Opportunities for more concrete rewards may not arise as frequently, but take full advantage of them when they do. If promotions or raises are within your power to give, be as generous as the circumstances justify, and take the occasion for telling the individual why you think he deserves it. If there is some criticism to be given, or suggestion for still further improvement, save it for a while. Let him have the full glory of the triumph for a few weeks, undiluted. After the initial euphoria has worn off, a serious discussion about the future, including any criticisms, will have more positive results.

If raises and promotions are not within your power to give, your recommendations will probably have weight, either officially at a scheduled review and report session or unofficially. If there is an opening thal would mean advancement for one of your team members, and you think he is qualified for it, go to bat for him with the boss. On written reports that will become part of a permanent file, be as generous with your praise and as sparing with your criticism as you possibly can be and still keep a clear conscience. Many organizations have the rule that such reports must be shown to the individual; it is a good idea to do so even if it isn't strictly required.

### Mediating and Moderating

The necessity for stepping in to settle a dispute between two individuals, or between a staff member and management, will arise much less often on a project team in data processing than in a factory or among clerical workers, But it could happen from time to time that you are faced with an irate team member who has a gripe or a grudge, or with a personality clash between two team members, which flares up into open hostility and endangers the progress of the project. You must take some action, and you must do it fairly quickly.

The first step is to get as much information as you can, remembering that it is not possible to ever be sure of having found out everything. If there is a dispute between two people, listen to both sides, preferably one at a time to avoid escalation. Check the facts as closely as possible, with reference to third parties or to any documentation that may have a bearing on the situation. Also, find out what company policy has to say about the circumstances, if anything. For example, in some organizations it is an inflexible rule that any physical violence must be dealt with by instant dismissal of those involved. If an operator and a programmer come to blows, both must be fired on the spot, regardless of the rights and wrongs, There may be a policy or a percedent that will help you in the present situation, but if you are at all unsure, consult with your boss.

Settle the matter quickly. This doesn't mean it has to be done on the spot. If you have listened to both sides, but want to get more information elsewhere, or if you want to sleep on it, do so. It will help if you tell the disputants what you are doing and name a time when a decision will be reached. Once you have all the facts, take one day to think it over if you wish, but try not to delay longer than that. If, for example, you want to try to effect a reconciliation, call the individuals into your office as soon as possible to ask them to shake hands. The longer they spend glaring at each other from across the office, the more difficult it will be for them to bury the hatchet. If the possibility of a dismissal exists, you owe, it to the person involved not to keep him in suspense any longer than absolutely necessary.

If the grievance is about you, if a team member comes to you to complain that you have not treated him fairly, first be thankful that he thinks enough of you to speak to you first rather than going over your head. Listen to his side and consider whether there is merit to his feelings. Before leaping to defend yourself, take a day to think it over and tell him that is what you are doing. If you them decide that his complaint is not justified, telling him so will have more weight. If there is danger of open hostility or if an equitable settlement seems unlikely, refer it to your boss. This is known as "passing the buck," but in some situations it is the best thing you can do.

**Skill Upgradation**

There are a number of reasons why you as a project leader should be concerned about education and training for members of the team. The most obvious one is that it will provide them with skills that will contribute directly to the success of the project. In addition, it will enhance their promotion prospects and advance their careers, long-term goals but important ones. Seeing to it that education and training are made available is one of the activities associated with the project leader's need to give help and support.

Methods of training are:

1. On-the-job.
2. Apprenticeship.
3. Formal courses.
4. Reading.

The on-the-job or trial-and-error method is the slowest but the most effective training device. It can also be most expensive for the company, which may have to live with and pay for mistakes made by systems analysts and programmers for the life of the computer system. But the lessons that are learned stay learned. One does not learn nearly as much from successes as from failures. Much education in data processing must be on the job, if only because of the pioneering nature of many of the projects that are undertaken.

Although there are no formal apprenticeships as such in data processing, the concept can be used to great advantage. A trainee or junior member of the team can be assigned an official adviser who is responsible for guiding his work and to whom he can turn for help. The idea can be expanded to include the more experienced staff; for example, assigning as an adviser someone more experienced in the application area or the programming language to be used, or someone who has worked on a similar project for a previous employer. The adviser need not necessarily be on the project team. For trainee programmers, it is often the chief programmer; for systems analysts it may be a more senior analyst; and even for the project leader himself, it may be a more experienced leader of another team.

There are any number of formal courses offered by computer manufacturers and by consultancy and training companies of programmers, systems analysts, and project managers. The personnel department, or other administrative department within the company, should be responsible for evaluating the courses available and planning a formal training programme for each individual. In some companies, though, this duty is neglected. If that is the case, it is even more necessary for the project leader to find out what available courses would be of value, especially to the project in hand, and to push management to allow his staff to attend them. Pressure of work is often the excuse for neglecting training; building courses into the project schedule from the start can help overcome this.

In addition to, or as an inevitable substitute for, formal training, a programme of reading can be of value. There are some very well-written technical books on the market, and many more that are not particularly well written but whose content may justify the effort involved in studying them. There is also an enormous assortment of periodical literature in data processing. Consultancies and software and programming houses estimate that professional staff need to spend at least a half-day a week reading or at least browsing through books and magazines in order to keep technically up to date in the field. In a commercial organization, this may have to be done on the individual's own time, but it is necessary for anyone who ie serious about his career. A department library, or even a project team library with books loaned by individuals, will help.

A supplemetal source of training is a programme of short talks by experts on technical subjects. If a member of the team, or some other member of the department has specialized knowledge of a certain technical subject that others could benefit from, a semiformal talk of an hour to an hour and half, with time for questions and answers, should be arranged. Another source of speakers is the computer manufacturer. If the team needs orientation to the application area at the beginning of a project, a user manager is ofter only too pleased to donate an hour or two.

**Summary**

The emphasis in this chapter has been on the style of behaviour of the ideal project leader rather than on his personality. Nevertheless, there are two personal attributes that characterize any good manager, and ones that cannot be learned from any book or course of training. They are experience and maturity, which only time can bring.

On the way to acquiring experience and maturity there are things that a project leader can do to improve his managerial ability. First, he ask advice of others, particularly his superiors. Being taken under the wing of an experienced and articulate manager, who wlll give advice and assistance as needed, is about the best thing that can happen to anyone aspiring to a career in management. Secondly, he can watch hcw other managers work and learn from their successes and mistakes.

Working for, or alongside, an appallingly bad manager can be as educational as working for a very good one: Finally, he can analyze his own mistakes to find out why they occurred and how they can be avoided in the future. A formal project-control methodology is of great help in this, and it is to that subject that Part II is devoted.

# 13

# PROJECT TEAM FOR DATA MANAGEMENT

## Team Structure and Order

The organization of the data processing department affects the way in which project work is carried out. This is usually determined when the department is first set up, but reorganization may take place from time to time. For example, when a new data processing manager is installed, or during a period of major expansion of the department to handle new systems projects, some adjustments may be required.

There are three basic patterns of departmental organization: hierarchical structure, pool structure, and permanent team structure. There may be variations within each of these, depending on local history and requirements. The three major types will be discussed in turn.

The organization pattern of this structure type is illustrated in Fig 13.1. This is a straightforward hierarchy, with the data processing manager at the top. He may report to a manager of management services, the chief accountant, a director of the company, or a divisional manager. The operations department, which includes data preparation, data control, and computer

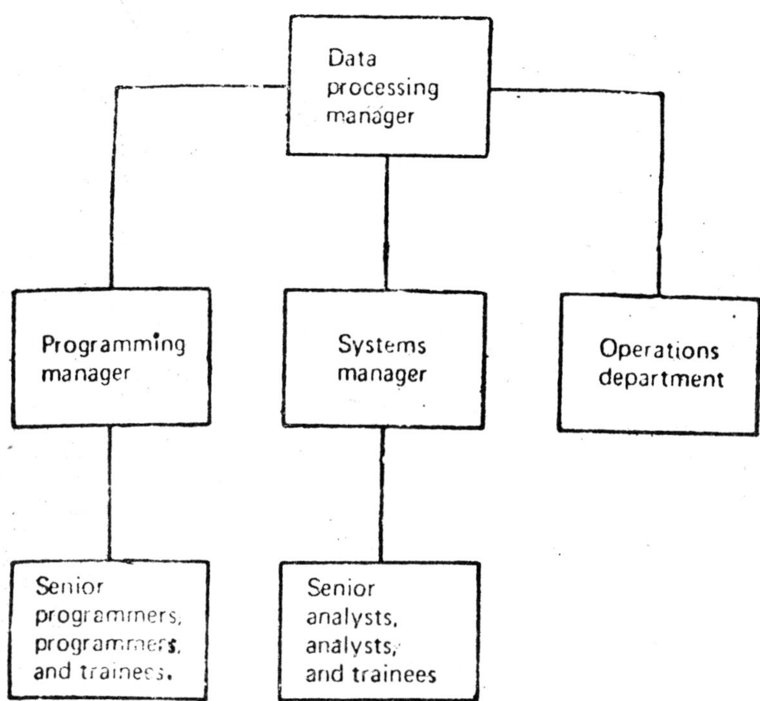


**Figure 13.1** Data proccessing department: hierarchical structure

operations, is shows on these organization charts for the sake of completeness, although it does not figure in the present discussions. Reporting to the data processing manager are a systems manager and a programming manager, who are in turn responsible for the analysts and programmers, respectively, and trainees in each category,

There are no teams as such in this type of organization. Individual analysts and programmers are interchangeable units. Each person is responsible to his manager for the work he is assigned. At least in theory he has no need to consult with anyone else about work in progress. Assignments are made from the top down on a "who's free next?" basis. One individual may be working on several unrelated projects at the same time.

This traditional hierarchy gives a very strong chain of command from the top down, perhaps through several layers of managers in large departments. The department can be urn as a "tight ship," with day-by-day control by management. This organization pattern is favoured by, and seems to foster, an autocratic style of management. Communication tends to be one-way only from the top down; even though "delegation" and "sharing of responsibility" and "team spirit" may be buzz-words frequently used by management, they are rarely put into practice. Data processing departments with this structure are often characterized by high turnover of staff and frequent complaints from staff about the quality of management.

If this type of structure is to be successful, documentation and work hand-over procedures must be impeccable and rigidly enforced. If they are not, strong informal lines of communication will develop, and in extreme cases will expand to include unofficial project teams. When this happens, the so-called "teams" usually spend as much effort in trying to thwart management as they do in developing systems. A totally autocratic manager may deny all informal communication between members of his staff, especially between analysts and programmers. Thus, if a programmer needs clarification of a programme specification, he must ask the programming manager who then talks to the systems manager, who then requests the analyst to provide the information, who then passes it back to the programmer by the same route. Needless to say, there is no known case of this regimen's working successfully.

The hierarchical organization may be the best oue for a small department with several projects running concurrently, since there may not be enough people to make teams possible. The whole department will run as a team, with many informal lines of communication between various individuals. The structure may also be favoured when there are rigid timetables and strict day-to-day control is required. In such a situation, it may be necessary to pay above-average salaries in an attempt to retain qualified staff; otherwise, there will always be a high turnover and a large proportion of trainees. Finally, this structure is obviously well suited for a military organization.

**Format for Action**

Figure 13.2 shows a typical organization structure with teams drawn from pools of systems analysts and programmers. The formal organization is similar to that of the hierarchical structure. A project team is formed for each new project, drawing from the pools of analysts and programmers as needed. The project leaders are usually experienced analysts, although senior programmers may sometimes be leaders. In the most fluid of arrangements, one individual may be leader for one project, but may also be a team member cooperating with someone else on another project, simultaneously or consecutively. Usually, however, the title "project leader" or "team leader" goes with the job, and it would be considered a demotion if one project leader were asked to report to another project leader. The size and composition of the team often varies through the life cycle of the project, with programmers being assigned to the team only when the analysts have finished the specifications and some of them have dropped out at that time.

A further variation in this structure keeps systems analysts and programmers separate. A project team consists only of analysts or only of programmers, with the work passing from the analyst team to the programmer team, and back again for system stesting and implementation. Informal communication will be required between the two groups, especially at hand-over stages. Further comments about this division of workwill be made later in the section "Systems versus Programming Teams."

The pool method of organizing work attempts to overcome some of the disadvantages of the hierarchical structure while

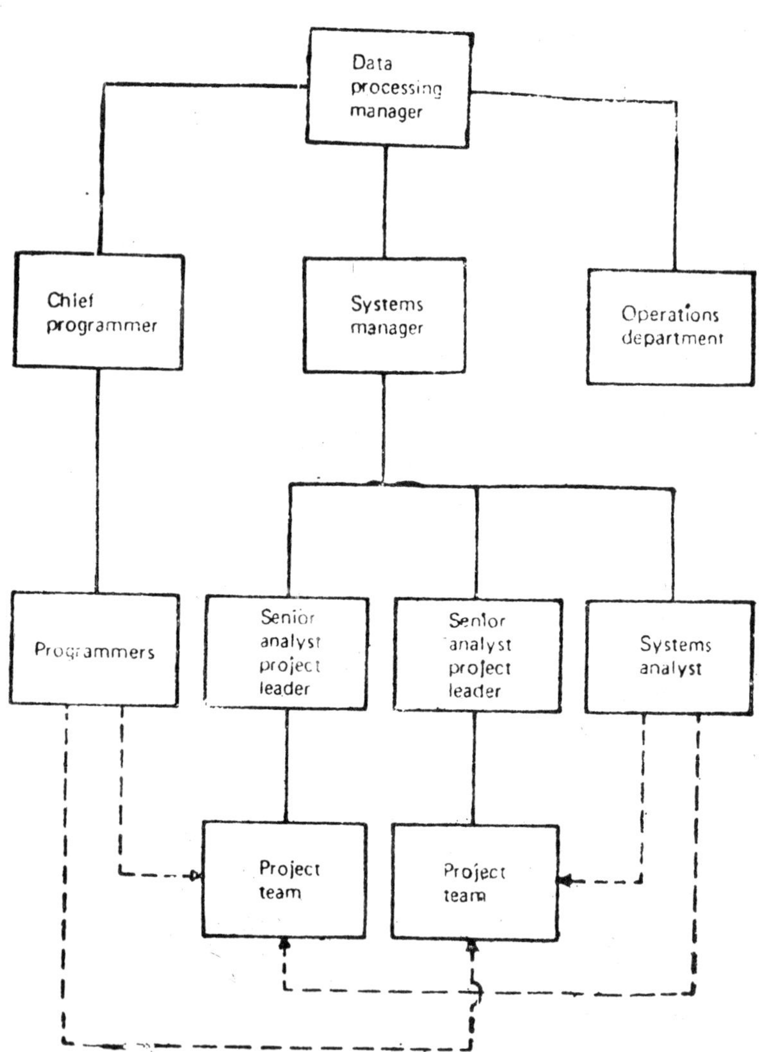


**Fig. 13.4** Data processing development: pool structure

retaining its strong points. Individuals can still be treated as interchangeable units to a certain extent, giving flexibility in assigning work. It is especially good for training strong project leaders and managers, for each leader can be given projects of increasing complexity, size, and scope as he gains experience. Some, but not all, of the advantages of permanent team are also present. A team spirit can develop, with individuals supporting and helping each other, and working toward common goals, but this effect is somewhat diluted as old members leave and new ones are assigned.

The major drawback of this method of organization is that it splits the lines of reporting. A programmer, for example, is responsible to his manager or chief programmer *and* to his project leader at the same time. This can cause confusion about who is really "the boss," especially if conflicting goals are set. For example, the programming manager may stress fast programme development to keep up the averages of his staff, whereas the team leader may be more concerned with the elegance of the output in order to please the user. These two goals are almost entirely mutually exclusive, and the programmer will find himself torn between two sets of loyalties. In extreme cases, the conflict may erupt into an open battle between the team leader and the chief programmer, with unfortunate results not only for the individuals but also for the project.

Other disadvantages include the possibility of competition between team leaders for staff members assigned to them. Each leader will want the best programmers and analysts for his team, quite naturally. A similar conflict may result when a team member is finishing work on one project and starting on a new one with a new project leader. Hostility between project leaders can lower morale on both teams, and in extreme cases their manager may need to arbitrate their differences.

Finally, there is the problem of breaking up the team as the project nears completion. Especially with a successful team will both members and leader resist. Tactics include delaying the project to keep the team together longer or political machinations may be put in motion to get a new project for the team without splitting up. This is a double-edged sword, for management may well want to consider whether it is desirable to dissolve a team that is successful and whose members enjoy working together.

## Core Structure

The permanent team structure differs from the previous two (hierarchical and pool) in that project leaders report directly to the data processing manager without the intervening layer of programming and systems managers, as illustrated Fig 13.3. In a large department, there may be a layer of project managers between the data processing manager and the team leaders. Each team consists of programmers and analysts, who are assigned to that team permanently. Transfers may occasionally

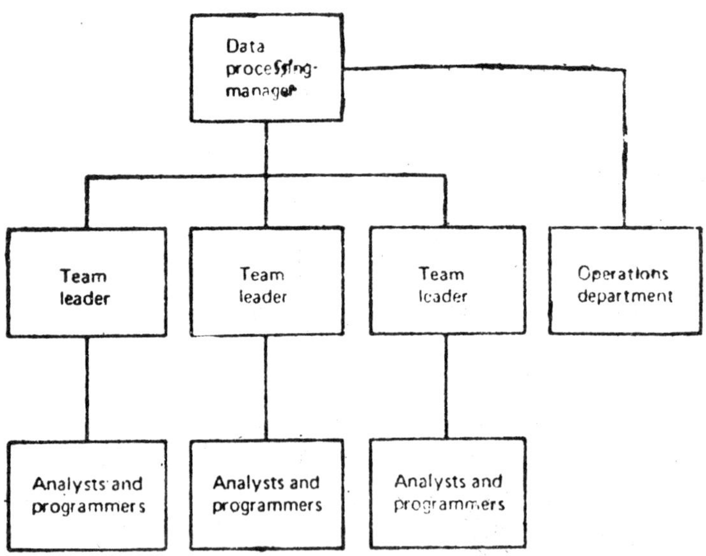


**Figure 13.3** Data processing department permanent team structure

occur because of personality clashes or overriding considerations of project priorities, but these are the exception rather than the rule. Teams may be dedicated to, and specialize in, particular application areas; for example, in an insurance company, there may be a life systems team, fire and accident team, and so on: or in a large retail organization, there may be accounts, sales and inventory, purchasing etc.

The advantages of permanent terms are strong ones if the project leader is competent. The group is a cohesive unit, with each member helping and supporting the others. There are common goals, attitudes, and standards that strengthen the team spirit. There is scope for individuals to develop specialist roles, both in terms of systems and programming expertise, and of group guidance. One person may be the taskmaster, oriented toward production and getting the work done while another is the team welfare officer, giving psychological support and smoothing over conflicts, (Ideally, both roles will be combined in the person of the project leader, but if he is weak in one or the other, an unofficial assistant will usually step in to fill the the gap.) Other useful roles individuals may adopt are the group humorist, the mother, the expediter, the clarifier, the secretary, the documentation expert, and the realist (or, as the others may see him, the pessimist.) A family atmosphere develops, with each team member feeling personally responsible for the work of each of the others and the team as a whole.

A successful permanent team has higher productivity and lower turnover of members than does the staff in either of the other organization structures.

The drawbacks can be numerous, however. First, the effectiveness of the team depends on a competent project leader. If he cannot knit the group together and guide their efforts, morale will plummet and resignations will be frequent—there is no other way to escape from the team. Even with an effective team, however, management may find that there is too much inflexibility in assigning work. When the team finishes one project, there must be another in the wings worthy of their efforts; ideally, each project should be more challenging than the last to make full use of the team's expertise and experience. It is not always possible to conjure up new work to these specifications.

Other disadvantages include the possibility that the common goals set by the group will not coincide with the goals of management. A team can work against management as well as for it, especially if their immediate manager, or sometimes the managers in the user areas, are ineffective. The family atmosphere may also make it difficult for a newcomer to be accepted, especially if he is replacing someone with seniority. (A young trainee, however, if properly respectful, may become the group darling.)

Finally, there is the possibility that if one member of the group decides to change employment, the others will follow him. They may not all go to the same new employer, but the psychological effect of the breakup will induce others to leave.

**Systems versus Programming Teams**

So far, we have considered only the vertical division of assignments, based on the organization chart. There are also a number of ways in which the programming tasks and systems tasks can be split within the department. The basic patterns are:

1. Systems and programming separate, with a traditional hierarchy.
2. Systems and programming separate, combination teams formed from pools.
3. Systems and programming separate, separate teams formed from pools.
4. Systems and programming carried out by the same individual, teams formed from pools.

5. Systems and programming carried out by the same individual, permanent teams.

The first approach is typical of the traditional hierarchy, and has already been described in detail. The second method is the one implied in the organization chart in Fig. 13.2. Systems analysis and programming are distinct jobs, with individuals drawn from the two pools to make up the combined project team on an as-and-when-needed basis.

The third method is a variation of the second. For each project, there are two separate teams, one of systems analysts and one of programmers. The programmer team will probably not be formed until a large portion of the initial systems work is completed, although the chief programmer or the individual who will become the programming team leader should be assigned liaison duties with the systems team to ensure continuity and smooth hand-over of work for programming. While programming is going on, the systems team may be be reduced in size, but with some members continuing to finalize detailed plans for systems testing, file conversion, user training, and implementation, and to advise the programming team as needed.

With respect to work assignment, the two-team approach is the most flexible. It also overcomes most of the possible conflicts that can arise with split lines of reporting. On the other hand, a large portion of the job satisfaction arising from achievement may be lost. This is particularly true for the programmers, who see nothing of the beginning of the project and little of the final completion. It may also be true for some of the systems analysts who ore transferred to other projects after programming specifications have been completed. In a long project, it is entirely possible that of all the analysts and programmers who begin the work, not one remains on either team when the system is implemented. Never to have the satisfaction of completing a major piece of work is a prime source of frustration for many staff members in departments using this approach.

The fourth and fifth of the patterns outlined above use a different type of job specification; combining systems and programming in the same individual: the programmer/analyst, progalyst, or anagrammer (but please, not "anal/programmer"). This has one major advantage and one serious drawback. The advantage is that it is possible for the individual to participate in the project all the way through. He has the motivation that arises from having a definite, long-term goal, supported by the satisfaction of achievement of a series of short-term goals on the way, and is able to see a major piece of work through from early stages to completion. This can be an important source of job satisfaction and a prime factor in attempts to retain experienced staff. The drawback is that systems analysis and programming require entirely different types of skills, and perhaps even different personality types.

Programming is technically oriented, concerned with hardware software rather then people. Systems work requires assertive self-confidence in relations with people rather than the computer. It is unlikely that the two sets of skills (programming and analysis) and outlooks on life will be found combined in equal proportions in the same individual. A team approach, however, overcomes this disadvantage to a certain extent. Members of the team are able to balance each other's weaknesses, and individuals can develop specialist skills. For example, one person may be particularly good at soothing users and maintaining liaison on testing with the operations department (the "public relations expert"), while another knows the operating system inside-out (the "software specialist").

Another possible disadvantage of the analyst/programmer job category is that it may restrict promotion possibilities. This is not true if there are separate job categories of programmer and analyst, with analyst/programmer as an intermediate step from one to the other, but only large departments can support the three different categories, In any hierarchical organization, it is necessary to have enough job steps for frequent promotion of qualified staff. Let us take two extreme examples:

1. Trainee → analyst/programmer → project leader.
2. Programmer trainee → junior programmer → programmer → senior programmer → programmer/analyst → senior programmer/analyst → project leader → project manager.

Suppose that in each case the average time taken to progress from trainee to the highest level shown is five years, and that the starting and final salaries are the same. In that time, an individual working for company 1 will receive two promotions, while someone working for company 2 will have had seven. The job responsibilities, salaries, etc., are exactly the same; the only difference is the psychological one of recognition and promotion.

A multiplicity of job grades can be carried too for, but it is better to have too many than too few. Having good work rewarded with a promotion and new job title, with or without a salary increase, gives enormous satisfaction and provides visible evidence of progress. The only cost to the company is a slightly increased paper-work load for the personnel department, a small price to pay. Installations using the analyst/programmer job function should take care to build in a sufficient number of levels of job category to make frequent promotion possible.

The fifth pattern of team organisation is a permanent team with each member being an analyst/programmer. The pros and cons of permanent teams have already been discussed. It only remains to point out that a permanent team is usually workable only if the analyst/programmer job category is used for at least some of the team members, probably all. If there is an attempt to divide the two types of work between different members, some will be sitting idle while others are overloaded with work.

**Staff Strength**

The ideal size of a project team in data processing is four to ten members. All-systems or all-programming teams are best if at the lower end of this range, with combination teams at the upper end. A team in this size range is small enough to allow easy communication between members, but large enough for individuals to develop specialisations. There are differing advantages at the upper and lower ends of the size range. A smaller group (four, five, or six) reaches workable decisions faster, but a larger group (say, seven to ten) tends to have more ideas and can analyze problems better.

Smaller teams may, of course, be necessary for projects of limited scope. The smallest of all is the "one-man team," that is, one individual with an assignment not related to other work going on Many current concepts can be applied in modified from by a project leader who has only one subordinate, himself. Even so, it is useful if the one-man team has available an official or unofficial adviser, perhaps his boss, with whom he can talk over ideas and problems.

Two and three-man teams are to be avoided if at all possible. They usually emdoy all the disadvantages of a small team with none of the advantages. If a personality clash develops, its effects will be much more serious than if there were others to dilute and help smooth over the difficulties. On the other hand, if the members like each other, the paucity of multiple lines of communication tends to encourage development of social relationships, and the individuals become more concerned with each other's welfare and friendship than with getting the work done. In other words, a clique forms, probably with aims antipathetical to those of management.

If the group is too large, the law of diminishing returns sets in. Individuals find it difficult to establish personal relationships with each of the other members, so clique within the group or a pecking order will develop. Too many possible lines of communication make it difficult for each person to be familiar with the work of all the others, so the group advantages of mutual help and support are lost. In extreme cases, the group will divide into two camps, with conflicting goals, and hostilities may escalate into a fead of such magnificent proportions that no work at all gets done

It is, of course, entirely possible that a project will arise which requires 30, 40, or more individuals assigned to it at the same time. In that case, it is necessary to establish a number of project teams, each specializing in one aspect of the work. Each team will have a project leader reporting to the overall project manager, thereby reducing his span of control to one of reasonable size.

Let us take a real case as an example. The project involved the design and implementation of a large property data base for a city government. Twelve different city departments were to take part in the new system. A five-year plan was developed; the first phase was to take a year, and 29 systems analysts were involved. They were split into three task groups. Group I was given the job of hardware selection and installation planning, a new main-frame computer and over 100 terminals being required. There were five analysts on this team. Group 2, the largest, was responsible for information gathering from the user departments. There were 17 analysts in this group, and they were divided into three teams, each with a project leader. Teams 1 and 2 arbitrarily divided the user departments between them; each had seven members. The remaining three analysts formed Group 3, responsible for administration of the group, documentation control, and coding the interview results for analysis by computer. 'There was some interchange of roles between these three teams as the work load varied. Group 3 had the remaining seven analysts, and was responsible for systems design.

Thus, there were five project leaders reporting to a project manager. Communications were established by means of a formal monthly progress meeting with all present, and frequent informal get-togethers of the team leaders and the project manager.

At the completion of the first phase of the project, after the order for the hardware had been placed, Group I was disbanded, and its members were given other assignments. There was some resentment about this because the members wanted to continue with the project. Some of the members of Group 2 were reassigned to Group 3, the design team, which was then subdivided for the more detailed specification stages, Others from Group 2 were made project leaders for the separate programming teams that were then formed. A few resignations had occurred, and the vacancies were filled by promotion from within and hiring of trainees to fill the vacancies at the lower level. An effort was made to synchronize recruitment with the recognization of the teams, so the newcomers had no difficulty in being accepted. Throughout the project, timetables were met with deadeye accuracy, and morale and team spirit were high.

**User Representation**

For new systems development work, a user representative assigned to the project team for the life of the project can be an invaluable aid. His exact duties will vary, depending on the type of project and the company, but a sample list might be as follows:

1. Administration: making appointments for systems analysts with users, organizing meetings, etc.
2. Information: answering questions about the application area.
3. Decision making: giving approvals and authorizations for changes to specifications and at project checkpoints.
4. Liaison: carrying messages between the project team and the user staff, and interpreting them as needed.

To be a valuable member of the team, the user representatives needs to have three attributes. First, he should be knowledgeable about computers and how systems are developed and implemented. Secondly, he should be thoroughly familiar with all parts of the application area. Thirdly, he should have the authority to make decisions about all but the major questions that may arise, and should be able to do so without lengthy consultation with others in the user department. A representative who meets these criteria and is also enthusiastic about the project is worth his weight in gold. Unfortunately, such a paragon is probably so useful in his department that his manager will be reluctant to let him go over to data processing, even temporarily.

If a compromise is required, concede first on knowledge of computers. A weak spot here can be easily corrected by a course, a programme of reading, and/or informal education by members of the project team. In the on-the-job case, be sure to allow slack in the project schedule to compensate for the time the team members spend on training. The second requirement, knowledge of the application area, may be modified somewhat. If the representative has a good working knowledge of it, he can learn the rest as needed, but again the schedule must be slowed down a little. Without any authority to make decisions, however, his usefulness is doubtful. The project leader could probably do just as well by negotiating directly with user management himself.

More will be said about relationships with users later in the book.

**System Maintenance**

A large part of the work of any established installation consists of maintaining operational systems. Most systems analysts and programmers, unless they are very lucky or always change jobs in the nick of time, will on some occasion find themselves engaged in maintenance work. We will examine the ways in which this work can be organized, and the advantages and disadvantages of each.

The four approaches to maintenance work are:

1. Permanent team.
2. Rotating team.
3. Development team.
4. Whoever is available.

**Core Team**

A separate team or subdivision of the department is established to specialize in maintenance work and only that. This team may also be responsible for maintaining the installation's software, including the operating system.

A specialized maintenance group works very well if the installation is big enough to support a permanently assigned staff. Recruits for the section either are brought in directly from outside and trained as needed, or are transfers from development work. It is necessary for management to be absolutely honest about the nature of the work; trickery backfires. A cliche of data processing is that nobody wants to do maintenance work, but this in fact is not true. Positions may be more difficult to fill, and salaries above the going rate may have to be paid, but installations that have persevered in setting up a permanent maintenance team have found that staff are available who are willing and happy to do the work.

To be successful, permanent maintenance team must be well managed. There must be enough members in the group to eliminate the constant pressure that often exists during maintenance. It must be possible to plan the work, and there must be enough slack time to keep documentation up to date. Further, the maintenance team should have the authority to reject any new system that is not tested and documented to a predetermined standard. If the staff is forced to begin maintaining systems that are not properly debugged and documented, the group will deteriorate rapidly, along with the systems.

**Support Team**

Under the rotation scheme, programmers and analysts are usually assigned to maintenance over a six-month period. Members of the development team sometimes begin their six-month maintenance stint when their new system becomes operational so that they can guide it through the first few months.

The rotation method seems to divide the work load fairly. There are certain drawbacks, however, One is that the regular entrance and exit of members means that a large portion of their time must be spent on familiarization with the operational systems. Hand-over and orientation procedures may occupy as much as half the time of the team. Another problem is that the assignments are rarely truly fair. When one programmer's turn comes, for example, he may be in the middle of important work for a new system and cannot be spared; someone else who is due for rotation off the team, therefore, has to stay longer than planned. This obviously leads to resentment, and can be a major contributing factor to high turnover: "The only way I could get off maintenance was to quit."

A variation of this method requires new employees to spend the first six months to a year doing maintenance. The rationale behind this is that it familiarizes them with the work of the installation. The real reason may be that no one else can be persuaded to do the maintenance work. In practice the idea may be self-defeating. Trainees cannot be assigned maintenance work because they are so inexperienced in systems and programming generally that they may cause a major disaster. Experienced recruits, on the other hand, will be reluctant to accept a new job that puts them into maintenance immediately, with only the manager's promise that it is a temporary assignment. This illustrates the paradox of maintenance work: It is a difficult and challenging assignment, often requiring the exercise of considerable skill, and yet it is generally regarded as the least desirable of data processing projects.

**Progression Team**

The basis of this method is that the team that developed the system in the first place stays with it and is responsible for its maintenance forever after.

At first glance, there is a strong advantage here; no time need be lost in familiarizing new employees with the system. Those who know it best are always there to keep it running properly. What usually happens in practice is a different story, however. After an individual s first new system is completed, he will be spending, say, 15 per cent of his time maintaining it, and 85 per cent on a new project. After the second system, time spent on maintenance amounts to perhaps 35 per cent, and continues to increase until eventually all of the most experienced staff are spending full time on maintenance. This point never actually comes to pass, of course, because they will have been long gone to new jobs before it does. The installation must then revert to one of the other methods for maintaining systems.

When the other methods are badly planned and controlled, they often degenerate into this one. Whoever is on the lowest priority work gets to do maintenance as it comes along. This means that the maintenance is usually left until it becomes a panic job, and when the work is done it is poorly documented, making the next person's task that much more difficult.

As can be seen, none of these four approaches is ideal. The best choice for a small or young installation is probably either the rotating team or the development team. As the list of operational systems grows, with the department probably growing along with it, thought should be given to establishing a permanent team. But maintenance will always assume crisis proportions unless it is planned in advance and unless standard procedures exist and are enforced. Many of the techniques that will be described in Part II of this book can be applied to maintenance as well as to new systems development.

**Pulling Together**

Various concepts have been proposed that are connected with establishing and maintaining good working relationships and high morale in the project team. These will now be brought together and expanded upon under four headings: compatibility, common goals, elitism, and physical proximity.

**Compatibility**

Ideally, members of the team should be of obout the same age and have the same general outlook on life. We all tend to trust and like people who have the same life-style that we do, and we are usually suspicious of those who are obviously "different." A group of young people will tend to reject the one member who is much older than themselves; older people may be patronizing toward a younger one and not take him seriously.

There are many exceptions to this generalization, however, and sometimes it is difficult to predict whether the group will like and get along well with a certain individual. For example, in one closely knit five-man team, four of the members were socialistic in their political leanings, while the fifth was ultraconservative. The four were rather pleased with their "eccentric," and although they kidded him good naturedly within the group, they would defend him hotly if he was critized by an outsider. In another case, a team of young programmers was joined by a man much older than themselves. The younger men wore long hair and flowered shirts and were all "single swingers," while he was always dressed quietly and was a happily married father of four. The others affectionately called him "Pop," and grew to like him very much. Within a few months the group was consistently bettering all previous production records for programme completion.

In both cases, there were several things that all members of the group shared in common. In the first example, the ultraconservative was of the same age and came from the same social background as the other members of the group. "Pop" shared common values and beliefs with the others in his group, who came to look upon him as a father figure. They would go to him for advice about their personal problems, trusting that he would not act as a judge and would accept their goals in life as being worthwhile. In both groups, the members shared common beliefs about the work in which the team was engaged. They had common goals that were mutually agreed upon.

**Object-orientation**

The team have common beliefs and goals in order to survive and to function effectively. These are long-term objectives, short-term objectives, and shared standards and beliefs. Part of the job of the team leader is to ensure that the group recognizes that these exist. To do this, he should chart objectives in these three categories, choosing them as much as possible from suggestions made by the group.

*Long-Term Objectives.* These objectives relate to the completion of the project. They may involve meeting a specified target date, completing the work within budget, producing a system that meets its stated requirements when examined after implementation, or a combination of these. Successful completion of the project is the pot of gold at the end of the rainbow.

*Short-Term Objectives.* However, it is necessary to give the team a chance once in a while to look forward to long-term objectives and to savor in advance the anticipated victory. These are the stages at which the short-term objectives have been realiz ed. These smaller but still worthwhile rewards of reaching intermediate goals on the way to the pot of gold are also necessary. It is difficult to sustain enthusiasm for a reward that will come in the distant future without having some concrete accomplishment in the present. As one programmer once said, "What I really want is for someone to come past my desk once an hour, on the hour, and put down the money I've earned for that hour's work." Short-term goals do not need to be set on an hourly basis, but within a time span of weeks. These can be tied to project phases and tasks within phases; completion of a programme or completion of an item of documentation, for example. Recognition and praise for a good job, especially one that is better than average or better than anticipated in the circumstances, can also be associated with attainment of these more immediate objectives.

*Shared Standards and Beliefs.* Shared standards and beliefs cover a wide spectrum. For example, they may have to do with the quality of the work produced, the importance of beating a previous record or the installation average, conformance to methods and documentation standards, or obstacles and difficulties that the group must overcome. Ideally, these should be compatible with the standards and beliefs of management, but sometimes they are not. For instance, a group belief may be that the user manager is an incompetent twit, or that data processing is not accorded its due importance within the organization. It doesn't particularly matter whether the beliefs are correct or not. As long as they serve to knit the group together without affecting efficiency or productivity, trying to stamp them out may do more harm than good. The project leader should not encourage an antimanagement attitude, however, if the group lacks some common tie such as this.

*Elitism.* One of the shared beliefs of the team should be that it is "special," a cut above the average in some way. In a well-functioning team, this attitude will probably emerge without any prompting from above, although the project leader may from time to time reinforce the belief by making reference to the importance of the team's expertise.

There is a wide range of possible characteristics that members of a team may take as evidence that they are an elite. They may be the most experienced group in the department, or have a history of past success, all marks of specialists. Their project may be the toughest one yet undertaken in the department, or the one with the most potential benefit of the company. They may be the biggest project team, or the smallest and most cohesive, or the most difficult to join. A reverse scale of values is possible, too: they may have the nastiest users, the most incompetent manager, or the lowest priority on computer time for testing; that is, they face greater obstacles than other teams.

Again, it does not matter whether the belief conforms to reality or not as long as all members of the team subscribe to it. If they believe they are elite, that probably makes them one, anyway. The only counterproductive beliefs are those that cause deterioration of morale and are in conflict with the overall goals of the company; if these spring up and cannot be changed, the only possible solutions are a change of management, dissolving the team, or both.

As far as possible, common goals should come from the group itself rather than be imposed on them from above. This is not possible for all objectives; for example, the completion date for the project is often set in advance, perhaps even before the team is formed. For short-term objectives, the group and individuals should be consulted and agreement obtained whenever possible. One way of doing this is to consult with a programmer at the time a new programme is assigned, and obtain his agreement on the estimated completion time. If he strongly disagrees with the estimate, serious consideration should be given to modifying it; otherwise, it is very unlikely that he will make an effort to meet the estimate.

The goals should be challenging but realistic. This means setting objectives that can be reached, but not too easily There should be a possibility of success so that the effort is not doomed to failure from the start; but there should also be the possibility of failure so that the reward of success will be sweet.

**Physical Proximity**

A project team should be assigned a working area that allows members to be within easy reach of each other. There are two reasons for this. The first is a practical one: The area layout must facilitate communication among members of the group. The second reason is the psychological impact: Rearranging the work area to make interaction possible reinforces the group feeling of being "special" and of being united,

As ideal arrangement might be one where each person has his own office, close to those of the others, with an additional project room that is especially designated for the use of the team for meetings and informal discussions. Economically, private offices are not always posible. If two or more share one office, outsiders who are not members of the team should be moved so that team members share only with each other. In an open-plan office, desks can be rearranged so all members of a team sit in the same area. In this case it is particularly important to have available a private room for meetings and talks, even if it is one that must be shared with other teams. If this is not done, the group will take to meeting in the men's room (making life rather difficult for female members of the team, or around the corner in the local coffee shop or bar. While this may foster the feeling of elitism it is not conducive to efficient working habits.

**Morale**

It takes time to build an effective project team. Merely saying to a number of individuals, "Right, you're a team; here is your project and these are your objectives" won't accomplish anything. The group may not reach its optimum effectiveness as a team for several months; it may take as long as a year if the members did not know each other before. This is, in fact, a strong argument against semipermanent teams drawn from a pool and in favour of permanent teams.

First, there are desirable characteristics of a well functioning group that are not necessarily indicative of high morale. These are neatness and orderliness, lack of conflict in the group, and high productivity. Although these characteristics can be developed through rigid discipline and coercion imposed by top management. they do nothing to prevent the team from being unhappy, frustrated, and totally devoid of group spirit.

Some of the signs that the individuals are working well as a team, with high morale and good group spirit, are:

—Members ask each other's advice and consult often to make decisions and solve problems.

—They defend each other against outsiders: "We can solve our own problems." "I don't care if Bill [a teammate] was right or not, John [not a teammate] shouldn't criticize him."

—There is a general feeling of optimism: "We can do it."

—Standing private jokes develop that are not comprehensible to outsiders.

—Members call each other by nicknames that outsiders are not allowed to use.

## Summary

This chapter began with an examination of the ways in which individuals can be brought together and organized into project teams within the data processing department. If there appeared to be some bias in favour of the programmer/analyst job category and permanent teams, it was not unintentional; installations large enough to support this approach usually find it is the most workable. There is a general trend in this direction, as well as in the direction of permanent programming teams and permanent systems teams.

There was then a discussion of the ideal team size, four to ten members, and the user representative on the team. This was followed by the subject of organizing staff for maintenance work, again with some bias in favour of the permanent team.

The chapter concluded with comments and advice about fostering a group spirit within the project team. This cannot be imposed from outside, but must grow within the team. To a certain extent, the growth of good morale can be encouraged by preparing a fertile ground, encouraging desirable tendencies, and discouraging undesirable ones. A number of passing references were made to the role of the project leader in this respect, The next chapter will examine this role in detail, with emphasis on practical advice for managing the team and its work load.